BRUCE LEE'S FIGHTING METHOD

BRUCE LEE'S
FIGHTING METHOD

BASIC TRAINING

by

BRUCE LEE and M. Uyehara

Poetry by Mike Plane

Forty-sixth printing 2001
ISBN-0-89750-051-2

WARNING

OHARA [P] PUBLICATIONS, INCORPORATED

SANTA CLARITA, CALIFORNIA

DEDICATION

To all the friends and students of Bruce Lee

ACKNOWLEDGEMENT

Our sincere appreciation to Joe Bodner, who spent so much time in photographing and developing the film. Our appreciation also goes to those who participated in this book: Dan Inosanto and Ted Wong. They were both Bruce Lee's devoted students.

To Rainbow Publications, Inc., for the use of several photographs taken by Oliver Pang.

Introduction

This book was in the making in 1966 and most of the photographs were shot then. The late Bruce Lee intended to publish this book years ago but decided against it when he learned that martial arts instructors were using his name to promote themselves. It was quite common to hear comments like: "I taught Bruce Lee" or "Bruce Lee taught me jeet kune do." And Bruce may never have seen or known these martial artists.

Bruce didn't want people to use his name to promote themselves or their schools with false pretenses. He didn't want them to attract students this way, especially the young teens.

But after his death, his widow, Linda, felt that Bruce had contributed so much in the world of the martial arts that it would be a great loss if the knowledge of Bruce would die with him. Although the book can never replace the actual teaching and knowledge that Bruce Lee possessed, it will enhance you, the serious martial artist, in developing your skill in fighting.

Bruce always believed that all martial artists train diligently for one single purpose—to defend themselves. Whether we are in judo, karate, aikido, kung fu, etcetera, our ultimate goal is to prepare ourselves for any situation.

To train yourself for this goal, you must train seriously. Nothing is taken for granted. "You have to kick or punch the bag with concentrated efforts," Bruce used to say. "If you are going to train without the concept that this is the real thing, you are short-changing yourself. When you kick or punch the bag, you have to imagine that you are actually hitting an adversary. Really concentrating, putting 100 percent in your kicks and punches, is the only way you are going to be good."

If you have already read the first volume of *Bruce Lee's Fighting Method (Self-Defense Techniques)*, this second book attempts to explain the secret of Bruce Lee's training method, how he developed his power, speed, finesse in footwork, etcetera. The next two books will cover the skill and application of his techniques. Most of the photos in this book and the next two have never been published before.

If you have not read *Tao of Jeet Kune Do* by Bruce Lee (Ohara Publications, Inc.), please read it. It was meant to complement this book, and the knowledge from both books will give you a full picture of Bruce's art.

Jeet Kune Do

Jeet Kune Do was founded by Bruce Lee
because he felt
the martial arts were too confined.

You can't fight in pattern he used to say
because an attack
can be baffling and not refined.

Jeet Kune Do was created by Bruce Lee
to show us
that an old art must transform.

Like the day turns to night and
night, to day
the way of fighting must also reform.

Bruce Lee developed Jeet Kune Do
but wished
he didn't have a name for it!

Because the very words, Jeet Kune Do,
already indicate
that it's another martial arts form.

Any form or style does restrict
and his belief is now in conflict.

Contents

CHAPTER I: The Fighting Man Exercise 14
         Stamina Exercise
         Warming-Up Exercise
         Flexibility Exercise
         Abdominal Exercise

CHAPTER II: The On-Guard Position 28
         Stances
         Balance

CHAPTER III: Footwork 48
         The Shuffle
         Quick Movements
         The Burst
         Sidestepping

CHAPTER IV: Power Training 66
         Punching Power
         Pulling Power
         Power Kicking

CHAPTER V: Speed Training 94
         Speed In Punching
         Nontelegraphic Punch
         Speed In Kicking
         Awareness

Sources:
Tao of Jeet Kune Do by Bruce Lee
Boxing by Edwin L. Haislet

Chapter 1
The Fighting Man Exercise

Stamina Exercise

Although you have the right attitude,
It's not enough to avoid a strife.

Although you have a heart of fortitude,
It's no assurance of saving your life.

You may have spent years in training
In the art of fighting you love so much.

But if you are winded in a sparring,
It proves that your condition is such

You need plenty of workout on the road,
Running two, three or more miles a day
Until your body can take more load.

Then comes a day you see the light,
You look up at the sky and then relay:

"Skill in performance is all right,
But it's not enough to prove your might."

BASIC TRAINING

Aerobic Exercises

One of the most neglected elements of martial artists is the physical workout. Too much time is spent in developing skill in techniques and not enough in physical participation.

Practicing your skill in fighting is important, but so is maintaining your overall physical condition. Actually both are needed to be successful in a real fight. Training is a skill of disciplining your mind, developing your power and supplying endurance to your body. Proper training is for the purpose of building your body and avoiding activities or substances that will deteriorate or injure it.

Bruce Lee was a specimen of health. He trained every day and consumed only the proper food. Although he drank tea, he never drank coffee—instead he normally consumed milk. He was a martinet who never let his work interfere with his training. Even when he was sent to India to find suitable locations for filming, he took along his running shoes.

Lee's daily training consisted of aerobic exercises, plus others which were patterned to develop his skill in fighting. He varied his exercises to avoid boredom. One of his favorite exercises was running four miles a day in 24 to 25 minutes. He would change his tempo while running—after several miles of constant, even strides, he would sprint several feet and then return to easier running. Between changes in running tempo, he would also shuffle his feet. Lee was not particular where he ran: at the beach, in parks or woods, up and down hills or on surfaced streets.

Besides running, he also rode an exercycle to develop his endurance, legs and cardiovascular muscles. He usually rode full speed—35 to 40 miles an hour continuously for 45 minutes to an hour. Frequently, he would ride his exercycle right after his running.

Another aerobic exercise that Lee scheduled in his routine was skipping rope, which you can adopt. This exercise not only develops your stamina and leg muscles, but also improves you, makes you "light on your feet." Only recently, physiologists have learned, by several tests, that skipping rope is more beneficial than jogging. Ten minutes of skipping rope is equivalent to 30 minutes of jogging. Both are very beneficiial exercises for the cardio-vascular system.

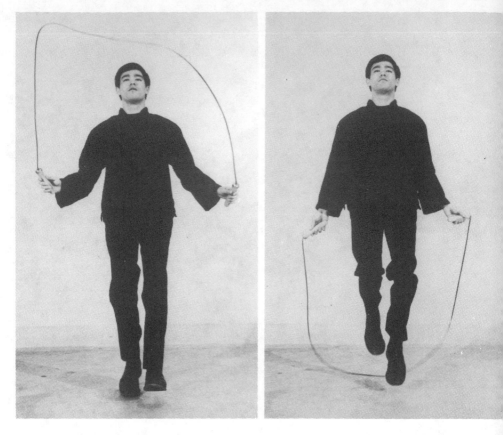

Skipping rope properly is one of the best exercises for developing a sense of balance. First, skip on one foot, holding the other in front of you; then rotate your foot, skipping on the alternate foot with each revolution of the rope, from a gradual pace to a really fast tempo. Minimize your arm-swing; instead, use your wrists to swing the rope over. Lift your foot slightly above the ground, just enough for the rope to pass. Skip for three minutes (equivalent to a round in a boxing match); then rest one minute only, before you continue for another round. Three rounds of this exercise are sufficient for a good workout. As you become conditioned to skipping, you can omit the rest period and do the exercise for as long as 30 minutes straight. The best rope is made of leather with ball bearings in the handles.

Additional endurance exercises are shadowboxing and actual sparring. Shadowboxing is a good agility exercise which also builds up your speed. Relax your body and learn to move easily and smoothly. At first concentrate on your form and move with lightness on your feet until it becomes natural and comfortable—then work faster and harder. It is a good idea to start your workout with shadowboxing to loosen your muscles. Imagine your worst enemy stands before you and you are going to demolish him. If you use your imagination intensely, you can instill into yourself an almost real fighting frame of mind. Besides developing stamina, shadowboxing increases your speed, creates ideas and establishes techniques to be used spontaneously and intuitively. Going several rounds is the best way to learn proper footwork.

Too many beginners are too lazy to drive themselves. Only by hard and continuous exercise will you develop endurance. You have to drive yourself to the point of exhaustion ("out of breath" and expect muscle ache in a day or two). The best endurance-training method seems to be a lengthy period of exercise interspersed with many brief but high-intensity endeavors. Stamina-types of exercise should be done gradually and cautiously increased. Six weeks in this kind of training is a minimum for any sports that require considerable amounts of endurance. It takes years to be in peak condition and, unfortunately, stamina is quickly lost when you cease to maintain high conditioning exercises. According to some medical experts, you lose most of your benefit from exercises if you skip more than a day between workouts.

Warming Up

To warm up, select light, easy exercises to loosen your muscles and to prepare them for more strenuous work. Besides improving your performance, warming-up exercises are necessary to prevent injury to your muscles. No smart athlete will use his hand or leg violently without first warming it up carefully. These light exercises should dictate as closely as possible the ensuing, more strenuous types of movements.

How long should you warm up? This depends on several aspects. If you live in a colder area, or during the cold winter, you have to do longer warm-up exercises than do those who live in a warmer climate. Longer warming-up is recommended in the early morning than in the afternoon. Generally, five or ten minutes of warm-up exercises are adequate but some performers need much more. A ballet dancer spends at least two hours. He commences with very basic movements, gradually but consistently increasing the activity and intensity, until he is ready to make his appearance.

Exercises

Bruce Lee learned that certain exercises can help you greatly in your performance, and others can impede or even impair your execution of techniques. He found that beneficial exercises are those that do not cause antagonistic tension in your muscles.

Your muscles respond differently to different exercises. During a static or slow exercise such as a handstand or lifting heavy weights such as a barbell, the muscles on both sides of the joints operate strongly to set the body in a desirable position. But in a rapid activity such as running, jumping or throwing, the muscles that close the joints contract and the muscles directly opposite elongate to allow the movement. Although there is still tension on both muscles, the strain is considerably less on the elongated, or lengthened one.

When there is excessive or antagonistic tension on the elongated muscles, it hinders and weakens your movement. It acts like a brake, causing premature fatigue, generally associated only with new activity—demanding different muscles to perform. A coordinated, natural athlete is able to perform in any sporting activity with ease because he moves with little antagonistic tension. On the other hand, the novice performs with excessive tension and effort, creating a lot of wasted motions. Although this coordination trait is more a native talent in some than in others, all can improve it by intensive training.

Here are some of the exercises that you can adapt to your daily training. For flexibility, place your foot on a railing or object as in photos A, B and C, keeping your leg horizontally to the ground—it could be slightly lower or higher, depending on your flexibility.

For the beginner, do not attempt any strenuous exercise.

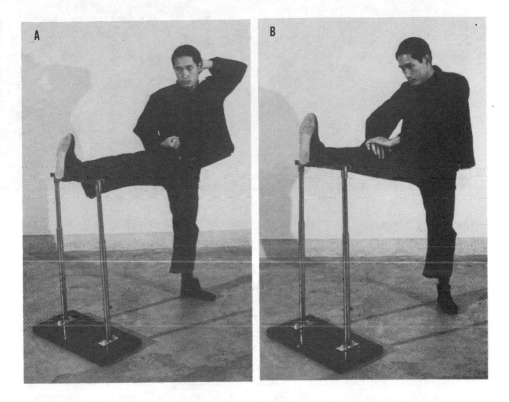

Instead, after placing your foot on the railing, just move your toes toward you, keeping your extended foot flexed straight as in photo A. After a few minutes, rotate your foot. In a few days, as your leg muscles are limbered, you can proceed to the next step, as in photo B. Press your knee to keep your leg straight and lean forward from the hip as much as possible without injuring your

muscles. From this exercise you then proceed to emulate photo C. Keeping your extended leg straight, push your hand downward. As you progress, you'll notice that you are also beginning to lean forward, putting more stress on your leg muscles. Finally you are able to touch your toes, as in photo D. After some months, you may be able to wrap your hand around your foot, as in photo E, even with the support raised higher.

Other leg flexibility exercises include leg splits and hanging leg raises, as in photo F. To do this exercise, use a long rope supported by a pulley. A noose encircles your foot. Pull the other end of the rope to the maximum height your leg muscles will bear without hurting yourself. Try to keep your foot horizontally aligned throughout the exercise. This exercise allows you to execute high side kicks. You should rotate your legs in all these exercises.

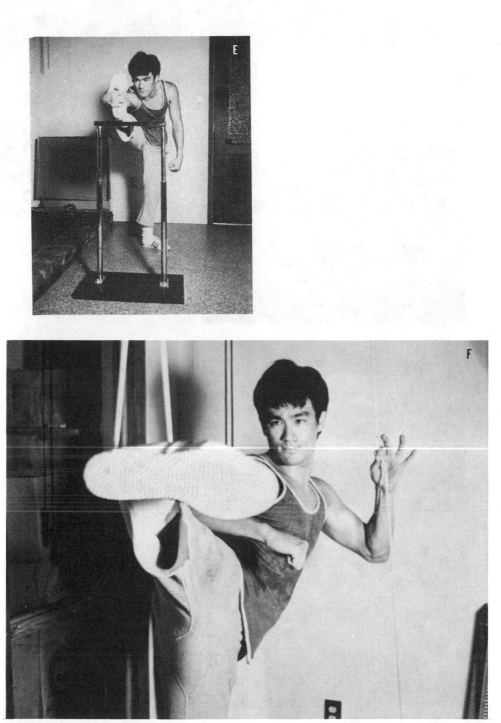

Advanced students who like to do exceptionally high kicking can progress into trampoline exercises. In photo G, Lee uses two light dumbbells and jumps high to develop both balance and springy legs. Once he can control his body on a trampoline, he attempts leg splits, as in photo H; a high front kick in photo I, and a flying side kick in photo J.

Other limbering exercises include body stretches. After you have developed elasticity in your leg muscles, you should be able to stretch your body as far back as possible, then bend forward as far as possible, until your head is touching your knees: photos K, L and M.

Abdominal Exercises

No one could help but notice Lee's abdominal muscles. "One of the most important phases of fighting," he used to say, "is sparring. In order to spar, you must be able to take punches in your midsection." To do this, Lee concentrated on several exercises that you can also adopt. The most popular are the sit-ups on a slant board, as in photo N (see page 26). Secure your feet, bend your knees and after placing your hands behind your head, lift your body toward your feet. Do as many as you can until you feel the strain around your abdomen. After reaching 50 to 100 repetitions, you can place a weight such as a dumbbell or barbell plate behind your neck and do your sit-ups.

Another excellent way of doing sit-ups is to sit at the edge of a bench, have someone secure your ankles, and lower your body as far down as possible toward the floor. This exercise stretches your midsection much more, but it is more difficult to do. If you have a chinning bar, you can also develop your abdominal muscles by hanging onto the bar with both hands and slowly lifting both legs until they are extended horizontally. Keep them in that position for as long as possible and try to beat your last record each time you do the exercise. Buy one of those kitchen timers to help you keep track of the time.

Another excellent exercise is the leg raise. Lie on the floor, keeping your back flush to the floor by pushing in your midsection, and lift your head slightly until you can see your feet. Keep your legs together and straight. Then lift them upward slowly and as high as possible. Then slowly return them to the floor.

To get the most out of this exercise, do not let your feet touch the floor—keep them about an inch above the floor and start to raise them again. Do as many repetitions as possible. If you have a weight lifting bench, you can do the same exercise as photo O. This exercise is also good for your lower back muscles.

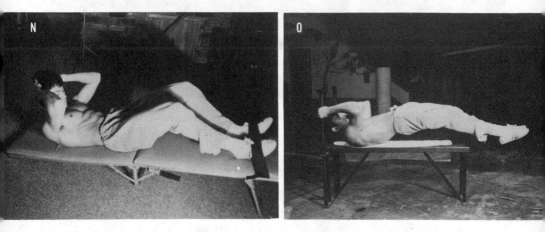

One advantage in doing an abdominal exercise, is that it can be done while you are doing other activity. For instance, Lee used to watch television while lying on the floor with his head slightly up and keeping his feet spread out and slightly above the floor.

To toughen your midsection, get a medicine ball and have someone drop it on your abdomen, as in photos P and Q. To vary your exercise you can also have someone throw it directly to your

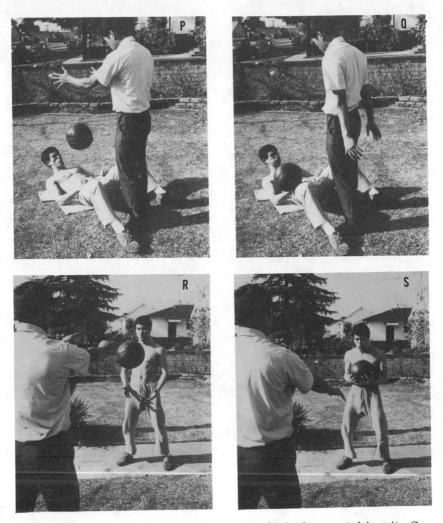

midsection. Let the ball hit your body before catching it. See photos R and S.

If you do your workout alone, you can use your heavy punching bag as a substitute for the medicine ball. Swing the heavy bag and let it hit your body. You can adjust the spot of impact either by moving forward or backward. If you want a heavier impact, swing the bag harder.

In your daily life, there's always an opportunity for more supplemental exercises. For instance, park your car several blocks from your destination and walk briskly. Avoid the elevator and use the stairs instead. While climbing the stairs, you can have a good workout, either by running up or by skipping a step or two.

Chapter 11
The On~Guard Position

A Perfect Stance

A stance too narrow provides you speed,
But leaves you imbalance which you don't need.

A stance too wide gives you power,
But you'll soon learn you're a bit slower.

There must be a stance that you can use
To keep you in balance and to refine.

The perfect stance that will not confuse
Is the on-guard position which does not confine.

You can maneuver with ease of motion
As you are free from any notion.

FRONT VIEW

SIDE VIEW

ON-GUARD POSITION

The most effective jeet kune do stance for attacking and defending is the on-guard position. This semi-crouch stance is perfect for fighting because your body is sturdy at all times, in a comfortably balanced position to attack, counter or defend without any forewarning movements. It provides your body with complete ease and relaxation but at the same time allows quick reaction time. From this stance the movement is not jerky but smooth, and prepares your next move without any restriction. It creates an illusion or "poker-body" to your opponent—concealing your intended movements.

The on-guard position is perfect for mobility. It allows you to take small steps for speed and controlled balance while bridging the distance to your opponent, and camouflages your timing. Since the leading hand and foot are closest to the target, 80 percent of the hitting is done by them. Bruce Lee, a natural right-hander, adopted the "southpaw" or "unorthodox" stance because he believed that the stronger hand and foot should do most of the work.

It is important to position your arms, feet and head. From the

INCORRECT

southpaw stance, the chin and shoulder should meet halfway—the right shoulder raised an inch or two and the chin dropped about the same distance. At this position the muscles and bone structure are in the best possible alignment, protecting the point of the chin. In close-in fighting, the head is held vertically with the edge of the chin, pressed to the collarbone, and one side of the chin is tucked to the lead shoulder. Only in rare, extreme, defensive maneuvers would the point of the chin be tucked into the lead shoulder. This would angle your head and turn your neck into an unnatural position. Fighting in this position would tense the lead shoulder and arm, prevent free action and cause fatigue because you would lack support of the muscles and straight bone alignment.

The leading hand position could be placed slightly below the shoulder height, as in photos A and A1 (close-up shot). In photos B and B1 (side view), pay close attention to the extension of both Lee's right and left hands. Photos C and C1 reveal another view of his stance from the back, showing his leading hand more clearly.

In photo Y, both fighters stand in the on-guard position incorrectly. The person on the left has his right foot too wide and reveals too much of his body. The person on the right has his right

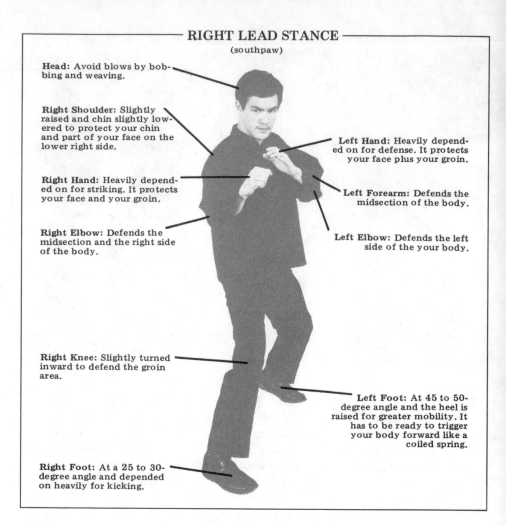

RIGHT LEAD STANCE
(southpaw)

Head: Avoid blows by bobbing and weaving.

Right Shoulder: Slightly raised and chin slightly lowered to protect your chin and part of your face on the lower right side.

Right Hand: Heavily depended on for striking. It protects your face and your groin.

Right Elbow: Defends the midsection and the right side of the body.

Left Hand: Heavily depended on for defense. It protects your face plus your groin.

Left Forearm: Defends the midsection of the body.

Left Elbow: Defends the left side of the your body.

Right Knee: Slightly turned inward to defend the groin area.

Left Foot: At 45 to 50-degree angle and the heel is raised for greater mobility. It has to be ready to trigger your body forward like a coiled spring.

Right Foot: At a 25 to 30-degree angle and depended on heavily for kicking.

foot too far to his left, restricting his movement and keeping him off-balance.

Sometimes, but very seldom, you can adopt the low-line position without a lead because many fighters are not prepared for such a defense. This type of position may confuse your opponent and severely hamper and, to a certain extent, check his offensive assault. Your exposed head is now a target but can be protected by mobility and relying on being a safe distance away from him.

The rear hand is held four to five inches from your body on the on-guard position with the elbow protecting the short ribs, and the forearm gently brushing your body, defending the midsection. The

Head: Avoid blows by bobbing and weaving.

Right Hand: Heavily depended on for defense. It protects your face plus your groin.

Left Shoulder: Slightly raised and chin slightly lowered to protect your face on the lower left side.

Right Forearm: Defends the midsection of your body.

Left Hand: Heavily depended on for striking. It protects your face and your groin.

Right Elbow: Defends the right side of your body.

Left Elbow: Defends the midsection and the left side of the body.

Left Knee: Slightly turned inward to defend the groin area.

Right Foot: At 45 to 50-degree angle and the heel is raised for greater mobility. It has to be ready to trigger your body forward like a coiled spring.

Left Foot: At a 25 to 30-degree angle and depended on heavily for kicking.

rear hand is aligned with the lead shoulder and placed almost to the chest of that shoulder.

The lead foot dictates the position of the trunk. If the lead foot is properly in place, then the trunk automatically assumes the correct position. It is important that the trunk form a straight line with the lead leg. As the lead foot is turned inward, the body consequently moves in the same direction, displaying a narrow target to the opponent. If, however, the lead foot is turned outward, the body is squared, presenting a larger target. For defense, the narrow target obviously is more advantageous but the square blends in better for launching some attacks.

A

Good form is essential in your stance. It allows you to perform in the most efficient manner with a minimum of lost movement and wasted energy. Eliminate the nonessential motions and muscle activity which cause exhaustion without gaining any benefit. Both of your arms and shoulders must be relaxed and loose, to whip out and snap your fists like thrusts from a rapier. Keep your lead hand or both hands in constant "weaving" motion, but always keep yourself covered while doing it. The lead hand should be constantly moving, flickering in and out like a snake's tongue ready to strike. This threatening motion keeps your opponent in a bewildering plight.

Remember, if you tense up, you lose your balance, timing and flexibility, which are essential to all proficient fighters. Although relaxation is a physical form, it is controlled by your mind. You have to learn, by conscious effort, to direct your thought and body into this new habit of muscular activity. Relaxation is a state of muscular tension. It is natural to have a slight degree of tension in your muscles when performing any physical activity. But your antagonistic muscles must retain a low degree of tension to perform coordinated, graceful and efficient movements. By constant practice, you can achieve this feeling of relaxation at will. Once you have acquired this, you should induce this attitude in a potentially tension-created environment.

Use a mirror to constantly check your posture, hand position and movement. Look at your stance and see if you are standing almost like a cat, with your back slightly hunched, chin lowered, with your lead shoulder slightly up and prepared to spring. Contract your abdominal muscles partially. Protect your sides with your elbows and leave no openings at which your opponent may hit. The on-guard position is considered the safest stance. In JKD it is the most favorable position for kicking, hitting and applying bodily force.

Some faults on the following stances:

A: Right leg is too far out and will hinder his movement, especially with the weight on his rear foot. With both hands on his hips, he leaves himself wide open for an upper body and head attack.

B: His stance is too square and he can easily be thrown off-balance. He is also restricted from deep penetration in his countering.

C: Elongated stance with long lead and extended foot places him in a vulnerable position. Lead side of the body is open to attack; extended hand is immobilized and withdrawing of the hand telegraphs his intention.

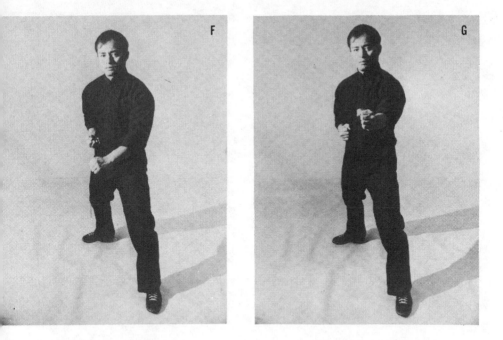

D: Both of his hands are too extended. His rear arm is held too high and leaves his body wide open. His front hand is too extended to deliver any kind of an attack.

E: Standing too much to the side prevents him from deep penetration for attacking or retreating. He can easily be thrown off-balance.

F: Both arms are carried too low, exposing his upper body and head.

G: Body is too rigid; lead hand is too extended for attacking and the rear hand is too low for protecting blows to the head.

H: Stance is too wide for any kind of mobility. It is difficult to attack without telegraphing from this position, and the groin area is exposed for a front kick.

I: Right arm is carried too high and leaves the rib cage area exposed. Hand is too extended to deliver any kind of an attack.

J: The cat stance restricts movements, especially sidestepping toward his right if he is in the right lead position. Secondly, any blow delivered from this position would not have power, because his weight is fully on the rear foot.

K: Stance is too narrow. It eliminates the springiness of his footwork. Knees should be slightly bent for the explosive and springy movement.

L: Like the cat stance, too much weight is placed on the back foot, and this restricts the forward mobility, especially with a wide stance. Tc launch a punch he has to shift his weight to the front foot and telegraph his intention.

M: Too much weight on the lead foot could throw one off-balance by a sweep. A too-extended stance is also vulnerable for a kick to the knee and shin.

N: With both hands on hips, body and head are completely exposed for an assault. The groin area is unnecessarily open because of the awkward placement of the rear foot.

O: This stance makes the body, face and the knee and shin of the lead leg vulnerable. Kneeling on the floor just about eliminates any mobility for attack or defense.

BIRD'S-EYE VIEW

Balance

Balance is the most important aspect of the on-guard stance. Without proper balance at all times, you will lose body control in the middle of an action. Balance is only attained with correct body alignment. Your feet should be directly under your body, spread apart at a comfortable medium distance, the space of a natural step, so you are braced and not standing on just one point. The weight of your body can be evenly balanced on both feet or slightly on your lead foot. By bending the forward knee, the center of gravity leans slightly forward, but the lead heel should have only a light ground contact to retain balance and reduce tension (light on your foot). The lead leg should also be fairly straight with the knee, not locked but relaxed and loose. Although the above rule is generally true, there is no fast rule that your heels should constantly be raised or flat. This depends on the situation

and position of your body.

The rear heel is raised to facilitate shifting of your weight quickly to the lead leg when delivering a punch. It also acts as a spring to your body. It gives in when taking a blow. Like the lead knee it should be slightly bent, but relaxed and flexible to perform. A good fighter is rarely detected with his knee straight, even when he has to move suddenly.

The on-guard position presents a perfect body balance which should be constantly maintained. The lead side of the body creates a direct, imaginary line from the front heel to the tip of the front shoulder, as in photos 1 (front view) and 1A (bird's-eye view). In photo 2, the side view of Lee's position reveals the natural distance between the feet, both knees slightly bent, with the rear heel raised a bit more than the front.

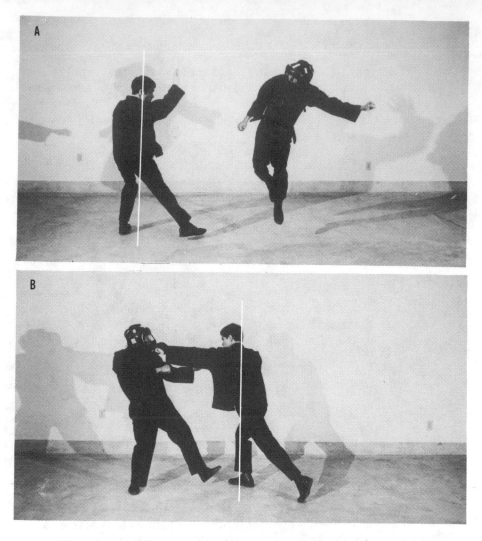

This stance allows you several advantages: speed, relaxation, balance and smooth movement, plus permitting you to unleash a powerful blow.

Good balance is controlling your body in any position—controlling your center of gravity. Even if your body is slanted or is placed in an unstable equilibrium—away from the base of support—you should be able to pursue and recover your equilibrium.

In photo A, Lee retreats from his opponent, maintaining good balance, and in photo B, he throws a long punch but still controls his body for any countering attack.

To control the center of gravity in motion, take a short step and glide instead of a hop or cross-step. To move rapidly, take several small steps. Take two medium steps instead of one long stride to cover the same distance. Your center of gravity constantly changes according to your own actions and those of your opponent. For instance, to advance swiftly, the center of gravity should subtly be transferred to the lead or front foot, unrestraining the back foot to propel your body to a quick, short and sudden burst. To retreat or move back quickly, the center of gravity should be transferred to the back foot, allowing you to be in balance for a parry or a counterattack.

Wide strides or constant switching of weight from one foot to the other in your movement, should be eliminated except in hitting and kicking. That moment of shifting results in poor balance and places you in a position vulnerable to an attack. Besides which, you are prevented from launching a strong attack. Additionally, you are allowing the opponent to time his attack at the moment of shifting.

You should strive for good balance in motion and not only in stillness. You must attempt to control your body with perfect balance, especially while delivering effective punches and kicks, because you must shift your weight constantly from one foot to the other. Retaining your balance while constantly changing your bodyweight, is an art few people ever master.

It is alright to switch your strategy while fighting or sparring but don't stray far from your basic form. In photo 1, the figure is

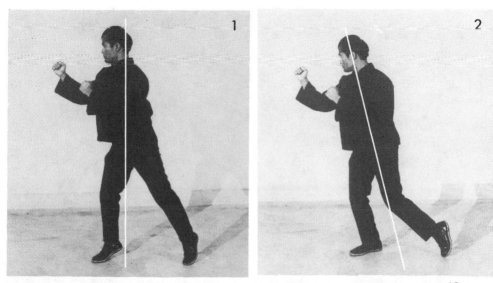

in fairly good position, slightly too much weight on his front foot. But as soon as he attempts to launch an attack, photo 2 (see page 43), he throws himself out of balance. Good form requires good balance. Proper balance and perfect timing contribute to good leverage, which is necessary to kick or punch with sustained power.

The most ideal position of your feet is one that permits you to maneuver instantly to all directions and serves as a pivotal point for your entire attack; one that keeps you in good balance to withstand blows from all sides, and at the same time furnishes you the ability to unleash unforeseen power in your blows. As in baseball, the drive and power in swinging a bat are derived from your legs, also.

The on-guard position presents you with balance and ease of movement by the proper body alignment. A too-wide stance, as in photo A, deviates from correct alignment, providing sturdiness and power, but forfeiting speed and efficient movement. A short stance, as in photo B, presents speed but loses power and proper balance.

Do not over-commit in throwing a punch or a kick—it affects your balance. Practice countering against a stand-up opponent. When he misses with a blow, he loses balance for an instant and is vulnerable to a counter. The only recourse he has, to be fairly safe, is to keep his knees slightly bent.

Learn kinesthetic perception or the faculty to feel muscle contraction and relaxation. The only way to develop this kinesthetic perception at first, is to place your body and its parts in different positions and be highly sensitive about them. For example, place yourself in a balanced position, then an imbalanced, feeling the contrast as you move forward, backward and to both sides. Once you have attained this feeling, use it as a constant guide to your body as it moves from gracefulness to awkwardness—from relaxation to tension. Finally, your kinesthetic perception should be so keen that you are uncomfortable unless your body functions with minimal effort to achieve maximum results.

To develop correct balance, practice from both the right and left stances, especially when performing the same tactics or exercises. Between training sessions, stand on one foot while putting on your clothes or shoes.

Practicing "chi sao" or sticky-hands-exercise is one of the best

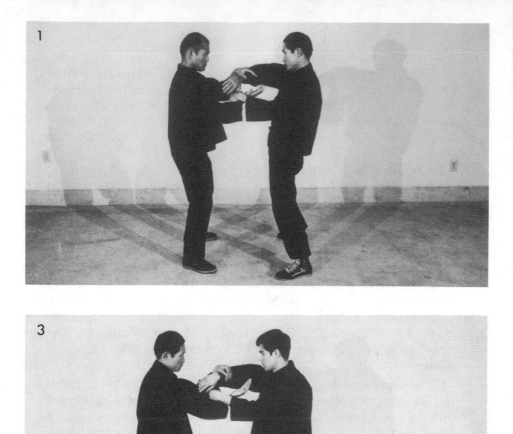

ways to develop balance. In the wing chun method, both practitioners keep their feet parallel to each other, as in photos 1 and 2. Both of their hands are extended until only their wrists touch each other. Each one, keeping one hand inside and the other outside of his opponent's, rotates his arms back and forth in a counterclockwise motion. Pressure should be applied to the arms in order to rock the partner from his position. To prevent this,

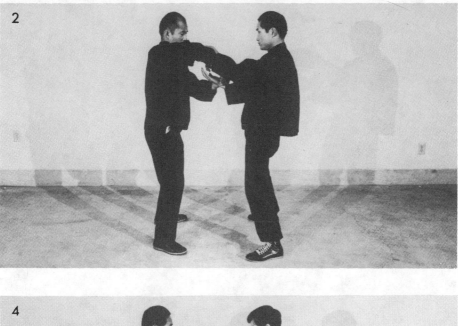

each should keep his knees slightly bent and keep the center of gravity downward by lowering his hips. In this position you have good balance from side to side but not back and forth. Eventually, Lee converted the stance by placing one foot forward, as in 3 and 4. In this position, one has a better all-around balance and this stance is not quite the jeet kune do on-guard position, but it resembles it more closely.

Chapter III
Footwork

Footwork

The art of mobility
  is the essence of fighting.

If you're slow on your feet,
  you'll be late in hitting.

A skilled fighter can shift
  to evade most blows.

His body is "light as a feather,"
  when he fights all foes.

He moves like a stallion
  galloping with grace

Instead of a kangaroo
  leaping high in space.

FOOTWORK

In jeet kune do mobility is heavily emphasized because hand-to-hand combat is a matter of movements. Your application of an effective technique depends on your footwork. Speed of your footwork leads the way for fast kicks and punches. If you are slow on your feet, you will be slow with your hands and feet, too.

The principle of fighting is the art of mobility: to seek your target or to avoid being a target. Footwork in jeet kune do should be easy, relaxed and alive but firm in movement, while the traditional, classical horse stance seeks solidity in stillness. This unnecessary, strenuous stance is not functional because it is slow and awkward. In fighting you are required to move in any direction instantly.

Proper footwork is good balance in action, which contributes to hitting power and avoidance of punishment. Good footwork will beat any kick or punch. A moving target is definitely more difficult to hit than a stationary one. The more skillful you are with your footwork, the less you have to use your arms to block or parry kicks and punches. By moving deftly you can elude almost any blow and at the same time prepare your fists and feet to attack.

Besides evading blows, footwork allows you to cover distance rapidly, escape out of a tight corner and conserve your energy to counter with more sting in your punch or kick. A heavy slugger with poor footwork will exhaust himself as he futilely attempts to hit his opponent.

The best position for your feet is where you can move rapidly in any direction and so you are well balanced to withstand blows from any angle. The feet must always be directly under your body. The on-guard stance presents proper body balance and a natural alignment of your feet.

The Shuffle

To advance, do not cross or hop but shuffle your feet. At the outset you will feel clumsy and slow but as you keep practicing this movement daily, you will develop your speed and grace. To do the forward shuffle, as in photos 1, 2 and 3 (front view), A, B and C (side view) and X, Y and Z (back view), stand in the

on-guard position. To move forward cautiously, slide your front foot forward, second photo (see page 51), about a half-step, widening the space between your feet just for a second as you slide your rear foot forward. When the rear foot is moved forward, you should be at the original position. Then to advance further forward, repeat the process.

Notice in the photos that Bruce Lee retains complete balance constantly and keeps his guard up. You should not be flatfooted in motion but should glide on the balls of your feet with sensitivity or feeling. Learn to move like a tightrope walker whose feet carry him safely across a high-altitude rope even when blindfolded.

Keep both of your knees slightly bent and relaxed. The front foot is flat but not heavily planted on the floor. It should be light and raised intuitively about one-eighth of an inch on a quick movement or sudden shift of the body.

The rear heel is almost always raised in stillness or in motion. It is raised slightly higher than the front foot, about one-quarter or one-half of an inch. The raised, rear heel facilitates switching your weight immediately to the other foot when delivering a punch. The raised back heel allows fast reaction of that foot and also acts as a spring, giving in to blows from any angle. Naturally, the heel should drop at the impact of the blow. There is no fast rule that your heels would be constantly raised or when they should be flat. This depends on several factors, such as your body position, your reaction to attack or defend—with your hands or feet, etcetera.

In the advance shuffle, you should be light on your feet and your weight should be evenly distributed, except for just a split second when you are advancing your front foot as in the second photo (—see page 51). At that instant, your weight would shift just a little to that foot.

In retreating or moving backward cautiously (see opposite page), you just reverse your movement. The basis behind the backward shuffle, as in photos 1, 2, 3 (front view), A, B, C (side) and X, Y, Z (back), is like the advance. From the on-guard position slide or shuffle your rear foot backward about a half-a-step, as in the second photo, widening the space between your feet just for a split second as you slide your front foot backward. When the front foot is in place, you should be in the on-guard position and perfectly balanced. Unlike the advance shuffle, your weight would shift slightly for just an instant to your rear foot, or the station-

ary foot when you slide your front foot backward. To retreat further, continue to repeat the process. Learn to be light on your feet continuously and keep your rear heel raised.

The forward and backward shuffle must be made with a series of short steps to retain complete balance. This position prepares you to shift your body quickly to any direction and it is a perfect position for attacking or defending.

Quick Movements

The *quick advance*, as in photos 1, 2, 3, 4, is almost like the forward shuffle. From the JKD on-guard position with your front foot (as in photo 2), step forward about three inches. This seemingly insignificant movement keeps your body aligned and helps you to move forward in balance. It allows you to move with both feet evenly supplying the power. Without this short step, the rear foot does most of the work.

As soon as you glide your front foot, quickly slide your back foot almost to replace your front foot's position as in photo 3. Unless you move your front foot instantly, the rear foot cannot be planted properly because the front foot will be partially in its way. So just before your rear foot makes contact with your front, slide

your front foot forward. At this position, if you have not taken another step, you should be back at the on-guard position with your feet apart at a natural distance. But the purpose of this movement is to move your body quickly to a distance, eight feet or more, that requires several steps. Except for the first three-inch step, the series of steps should be made at a normal walking space. This movement keeps your body in perfect alignment and allows you to move rapidly ahead.

In photo 3, it seems like Lee is in an awkward position, but he is in that position for just a split second. If you were actually watching him physically, you would have witnessed only a flowing, graceful movement and never detected any awkwardness.

Quick Retreat

The footwork for the quick retreat or rapid backward movement is almost similar to the quick advance except you move the opposite direction. From the on-guard position, as in photo A (see page 56), move your front foot back, as in photo B. The front foot, like the quick advance, initiates the movement with the rear foot following just a split second later. Unless you move your rear

QUICK RETREAT

foot before the front foot makes contact, the front foot cannot be planted properly. Unlike the quick advance, you do not have to slide any of your foot three inches. It is just one quick motion, but your body should be in alignment and in balance. If you were to move just once, you should be at the on-guard position when both of your feet are in place. But the purpose of this movement is to move your body four feet or more.

The quick movement and shuffle can only be accomplished by being light on your feet. The best exercise for overcoming the force of inertia to your feet is skipping rope and shadowboxing several minutes. While exercising, you must constantly be conscious of keeping your feet "light as a feather." Eventually, you will be stepping around with natural lightness.

You must move without any strain, gliding on the balls of your feet, bending your knees slightly and keeping your rear heel raised. Have feeling or sensitivity in your footwork. Quick or relaxed footwork is a matter of proper balance. In your training as you return to an on-guard position after each phase of maneuvers, shuffle on the balls of your feet with ease and feeling before continuing on your next maneuver. This drill enhances your skill as it simulates actual fighting.

Unless there is a strategic purpose, forward and backward

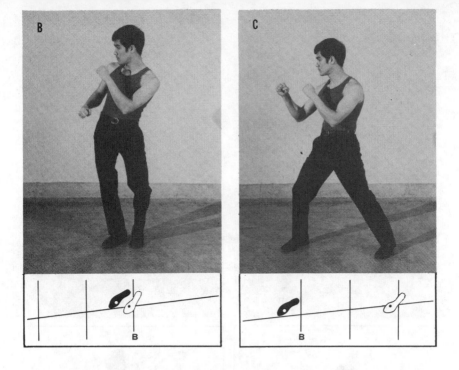

movements should be made with short and quick slides. Lengthy steps or foot actions which cause your weight to shift from one foot to the other, should be eliminated except in delivering a blow, because at that moment, your body is imbalanced—restricting your attack or defense effectively. Crossing your feet in motion is a bad habit as it tends to unbalance you and exposes your groin area.

The movement should not be a series of hops nor should it be jerky. Both feet should be slithering rhythmically just above the surface of the floor like a graceful ballroom dancer. Visually, your movement should not be like the kangaroo hopping across the open plain but should be like a stallion galloping with even, rhythmic and graceful strokes of its feet.

The Burst

The forward burst or lunge is the quickest JKD movement. It is also one of the hardest to learn because it depends on good coordination, and your balance can be thrown off very easily. It is utilized to penetrate deeply to attack with a side kick or to counter an attack such as a kick.

The forward burst is one deep lunge. From an on-guard position as in 1, step forward about three inches with your front foot, like the quick advance movement, to align your body and be in balance, as in photo 2. Then for faster reaction use your lead hand as an impetus. By sweeping your lead hand upward, a momentum is created, like someone is jerking you forward suddenly as you are holding on to a rope (see drawings A and B). This sweep of your hand also distracts your opponent and throws his timing off.

While sweeping your hand upward, your hips swing forward

simultaneously, dragging your rear foot forward. In that split instant, your weight is heavily on your front foot, only at this moment your leg straightens out to thrust your body forward. Sometimes, on an especially deep, penetrating leap, your rear foot may be ahead of your front while you are gliding in the air, as in photo X. You must land on your left foot only, as your right foot is delivering a side kick, as in photo Y. As soon as you have completed your kick, you should quickly place your right foot down and assume the on-guard position. That one leap should carry your body at least two wide steps.

In a recently conducted test, by using the forward burst, it took only three-quarters of a second to travel eight feet. By applying the classical lunge movement or stepping by crossing your feet, it took one-and-one-half seconds to reach the same distance—twice the time.

The leap should be more horizontal than vertical. It is more like a broad jump than a high jump. You should try for distance by keeping your feet close to the floor. Your knees should always be bent slightly so that the powerful thigh muscles (springy explosiveness) are utilized.

When practicing this footwork in the beginning, don't worry about your hands. Just keep them in the regular JKD position and concentrate on your footwork. Once you are accustomed to the feet movement with proper balance, learn to sweep your hand forward just before each leap.

Later, to develop speed and naturalness in your movement, adopt the following exercise in your daily training. From an on-guard position do the forward burst without penetrating too deeply by sweeping your hand upward, leaping forward without straining yourself, and quickly placing your front foot down without kicking. Continue to do this motion over and over again without stopping but keeping your balance and fluidity in motion. This exercise is excellent to adapt your body to move with ease, rhythm and grace. As you become more adaptable to the movement, increase your speed and work toward shortening the distance by more and more execution. Eventually, you can substitute a back fist punch for the sweeping movement of your hand.

The backward thrust is like the quick backward movement except that it carries your body backward quicker and deeper. From an on-guard position, push the ball of your front foot to initiate the motion which straightens your front knee and shifts the weight to the rear foot. Then the front foot, without pausing from the initial motion, leaves the floor and crosses your rear foot. Just before it lands, your rear leg, with its knee bent and acting like a spring, should thrust your body with a sudden straightening of its leg. You should land on the ball of your front foot just a second before your rear foot touches the floor. That one quick motion should carry your body backward at least two natural walking steps.

The backward burst carries your body just as fast as the forward lunge. In the same test it took exactly the same time to travel eight feet backward as forward—three-quarters of a second. But by comparison, the classical movement covered the same distance in one second flat.

For your daily training do the backward burst for speed, balance and rhythm instead of deep penetration. Move with lightness of your feet and keep practicing toward shortening the distance.

In between your jogging do a quick advance by rapid shuffling of your feet and then returning to your jogging. Another exercise is to practice with a partner. Let your partner do the backward burst while you do the forward. From an on-guard position, attempt to reach your partner with a light side kick as he tries to keep his distance. Then reverse your positions.

Learn not to hurl yourself recklessly at your partner but attempt to narrow the gap of space in a calm and exact manner. Keep drilling faster and faster by lunging two-to-three-hundred times per day. Acceleration can be increased only by discipline in your workout.

Sidestepping

Sidestepping is the technique of moving your body toward the right or left without losing your balance. It is a safe and essential, defensive maneuver to attack or produce openings for a countering when the opponent least expects it. It is used to avoid straightforward assaults, blows or kicks. You can also frustrate your opponent by simply moving when he is about to attack.

To sidestep to the right from an unorthodox (southpaw) on-guard position, as in photo 1 (see photos on page 62), move your right foot sharply, slightly forward and toward the right about 18 inches, as in photo 2. Your left or rear foot supplies the impetus as you land lightly on the ball of your right foot. For a split instant your shoulder sways toward your right and your weight shifts on the front foot with its knee bent. Your shoulder automatically realigns when you quickly slide your left foot in the exact manner and resume the on-guard position, as in photo 3.

To sidestep to the left from a southpaw stance, as in photo A, move your left foot slightly forward and to your left about 18 inches, as in photo B. During this motion your body is more aligned than when moving toward the right. Since your body is more aligned, you are in better balance and your weight is evenly

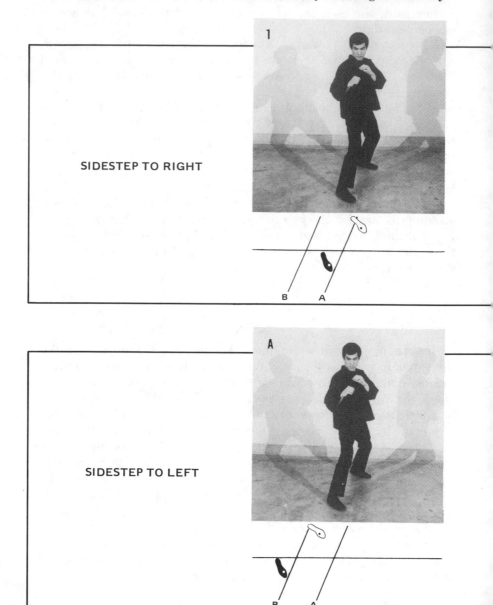

SIDESTEP TO RIGHT

SIDESTEP TO LEFT

distributed between the two feet during the shift. Your right or front foot should follow immediately in the exact manner, returning you to the on-guard stance, as in photo C. You will notice that sidestepping toward your left is more natural and easier than to the right.

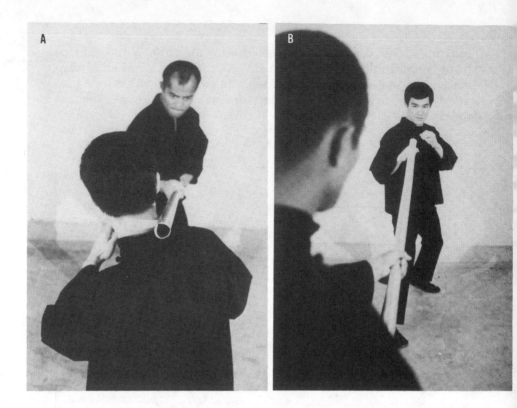

Bruce Lee uses a staff to practice his footwork. In photo A, he places the staff near his neck and slightly above his shoulder. The partner attempts to thrust the long staff at the exact area and Lee to adjust to the thrust.

In photos B and C (front view), the partner thrusts his staff and Lee sidesteps toward his left, keeping his body in balance and his eyes continuously on his partner. He has to move sharply to avoid the edge of the staff.

In close fighting or in-fighting, a fairly safe stance is the drop shift or the forward drop, as in photo D. This is done by shifting your body forward and slightly to your left, with your head in close and both hands carried high. It is used to gain the outside or inside guard position to enable you to strike the opponent's groin, throw an uppercut, stomp his instep or grapple him down. In the forward shift you can move directly to the left, right or back, using the same step. This depends on your strategy and the degree of safety required in that instant.

Against an orthodox fighter, you would sidestep to your right

or away from his rear hand. Against a southpaw, you move the opposite, mostly to your left. The art of sidestepping is not to move early but late and quickly, just before you are hit.

In nearly all motions, your first step is with the foot moving to that particular direction in which you intend to go. In other words, if you sidestep to your right, your right foot moves first toward that direction. If you sidestep to your left, your left foot moves first.

To move quickly, your body should lean toward the direction you are going just before you step out.

In jeet kune do, the aim of footwork is simplification, economy and speed with a minimum of motion. Move just enough to avoid the opponent's attack or blow, and let him commit himself fully. Do not tire yourself by dancing on your toes like a fancy boxer.

While practicing, stand naturally—with ease and comfort—so your muscles can perform at their peak. Learn to differentiate between personal comfort and drilling comfort. You should never be set or tensed, but flexible and prepared.

Chapter IV
Power Training

Power

Power in hitting
  depends not on your strength.

But it is the way,
  you throw your blows.

It is not whether
  you are close or at length.

If you're too near,
  use your striking elbows.

If you're too far,
  use your kicking feet.

But it is the hands that
  you'll employ the most

In a sparring session
  or a martial arts meet.

And when it is all over,
  hope you can silently boast

That you have learned
  to hit with speed and power.

POWER TRAINING

Power in hitting is not based strictly on strength. How many times have you seen a boxer who is not muscular but packs a wallop in his punch? And then you see another, heavily muscular boxer who can't knock anyone down. The reason behind this is that power isn't generated by your contractile muscles but from the impetus and speed of your arm or foot. Bruce Lee, a 130-pounder, was able to hit harder than a man twice his size, because Lee's blow with a heavy force behind it, was much faster.

In jeet kune do you do not hit by just swinging your arm. Your whole body should participate in the impetus—your hips, shoulders, feet and arms. The inertia of your punch should be a straight line in front of your nose—using it as the guiding point, as in photo 1. The punch originates not from the shoulder but from the center of your body.

In photo 2, the fist lands too far to his left, exposing his right side for a counterattack, and not allowing much time to recover for a defense. In photo 3, the punch comes from his shoulder with not much power behind it. He is too rigid to take advantage of his hip and body motion.

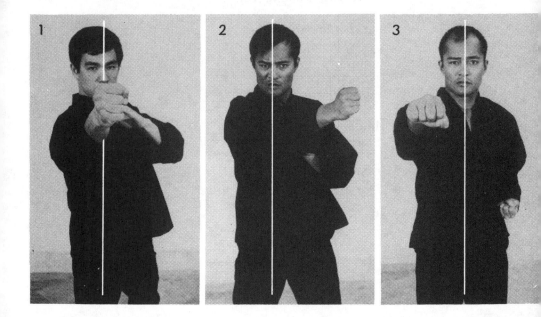

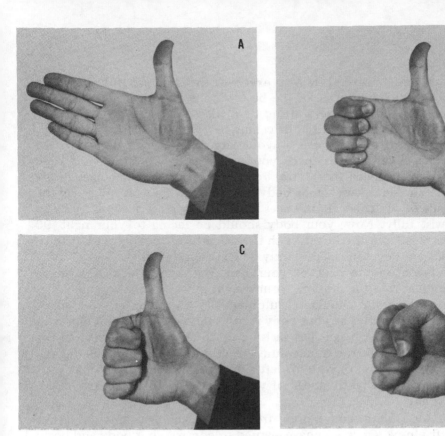

Punching Power

Straight punching or kicking is the basis for scientific and artistic fighting. It is a modern concept in fisticuffs derived from the knowledge of body leverage and makeup. A punch from your arm alone doesn't supply enough power. Your arms should be used strictly as bearers of your force; and the correct application of your body should furnish the power. In any power punching, the body must be balanced and aligned with your lead foot, forming a straight line. This section of your body is the mainstay, functioning as an axis to generate power.

Before you can punch with power, you must first learn to clench your fists properly, otherwise you are liable to injure them. From an outspread position of your fingers and thumb, as in photo A, roll your finger tips into your palm, as in photos B and C. Then overlap your thumb tightly over your clenched fingers. The tip of the thumb extends to the center of your middle finger, as in photo D.

There are several training exercises that you can utilize to learn power punching. One of the best ways is to learn the use of your hips. To do this, tie a string to a piece of paper, about 8 x 11 inches, and hang it from the ceiling to your chest height.

Using this thin paper as your target, stand about seven to ten inches away with both of your feet parallel to it. Keeping both loosely-clenched fists in front of your chest, elbows hanging freely at your sides, twist your body clockwise as far as it will go on the balls of your feet. Both knees must bend slightly for your body to twist fully. Now, your body should be facing to your right, 90 degrees from the target, with the weight shifting to your left foot. But your eyes must constantly be fixed on the target.

Pivot on the balls of your feet, with your hips initiating a sudden, rotating motion. Your weight quickly shifts to your other foot as your shoulders automatically rotate after your hips. Simultaneously, as your body is rotating, raise your right elbow to your shoulder height just in time to apply an elbow strike to the proper target. The momentum should turn your body 180 degrees so it faces the opposite or left side. It is very important that your hips rotate slightly ahead of your shoulders, to obtain maximum power.

Repeat the same motion from the left side, striking with your left elbow. Once you have learned to control your body and begin to feel at ease in this exercise, you may use your fists.

Step back about 20 to 25 inches from the target. Keeping your exact body position, swing at the target with a straight punch. At this point, your body should be aligned properly, you should have good balance and your motion should be fluid, with your hips initiating the rotation. Your power in the punches should have increased between 80 to 100 percent.

Gradually, to keep your body in balance especially after the completion of the swing, place your left foot forward and your right foot back (orthodox stance). From this position, twist your body clockwise until your shoulders are in a straight line with the target. Your front foot should be about 15 inches away. Now your weight leans heavily on your rear foot with both knees slightly bent. As the hips initiate the movement, you pivot on the balls of both feet, and your body is driven forward by the impetus from the rear foot. Your rear heel rises as your weight quickly shifts to the front foot with the delivery of the punch. At the completion of the action, your rear knee is practically straightened and your rear heel is almost completely raised. Your body should be facing the target. This motion is similar to a baseball player swinging his bat with all his might.

Once you have grasped this way of hitting, you can begin to work on your power blows by hitting the heavy punching bag, as in photo A. Here, Lee uses his elbow strike to develop his hip motion, then later works on his punches, as in photo B.

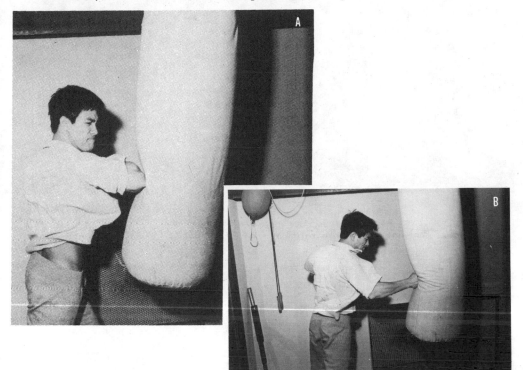

Your final step in punching for power is to reverse your footing and position yourself in the on-guard stance, with your right foot in front. With both of your knees slightly bent, rear heel raised, shift your weight just slightly to the rear foot for an instant. Your weight should be set for less than a second as you have to rotate your hips counterclockwise, and your weight switches to the front foot just before you throw a punch. This leading straight punch doesn't have as much power as the others, which have access to a freer and fuller rotation of the hips. But if you can master this punch with the right timing of rotating your hips, you have a

punch much more effective than a jab and very instrumental in the success of your sparring and fighting. It will be your most usable and dependable weapon. Like the other punching techniques, from the paper target you can substitute more solid targets to develop your power.

Lee used to concentrate heavily on the straight lead punch in his daily training schedule, using different apparatus. In photos 1 and 2, he uses a punching pad. Sometimes he drew his right hand back to throw a much heavier blow, as in photos A and B, to simulate close fighting.

Another apparatus used in his training was the light shield, as in photos X and Y, Lee liked to use various hitting equipment because he used to say, "I don't know the true feeling of hitting a person. First of all, each part of the human body has a different composition. You may hit a hard, bony substance or a soft, fatty area. And second, hitting with gloves on is different from bare knuckles. Unfortunately, using bare knuckles on your partner is not too practical."

The shield presents a different feeling when there is a contact. The shield is more solid than the pad and since the holder stands more firmly with both hands on the equipment, it will not give in, as the pad will. For a more punishing punch, Lee selects the canvas

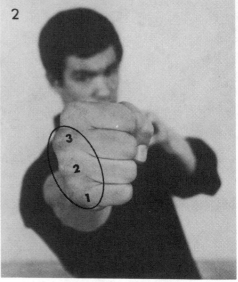

bag, as in photo 1. He usually had three bags hanging on the wall. One was filled with sand, another with gravel or beans and the third with steel sawdust found in any machine shop. In the beginning it is wise that you wear light boxing gloves on the heavy canvas bag as well as these wall bags. You must first toughen your knuckles before going bare-fisted.

In jeet kune do your punches are not thrown as the classical stylist's. Instead of using the first two knuckles (the index and the middle fingers), use the three knuckles, as in photo 2. The punches are not thrown from the hips in JKD, as the figure on the left, below, but from the chest as Lee is about to do in photo A. The delivery should be straight and not with a twist of your hand. If you twist your hand, the knuckles will align horizontally at impact but if you deliver straight out it will hit the target either vertically or obliquely, as in photo B. Consequently, you should toughen the three knuckles, as in photo 2.

Besides punching the wall canvas bags for toughening, you can also train with a sand or gravel box, as in photo C. Other exercise includes push-ups with your clenched fists. Place the knuckles of your index finger and the two small fingers on a hard floor so your palms face each other. This is an excellent exercise for beginners as they can gradually toughen their knuckles without risk of injury.

A

B

C

By being on the southpaw or JKD on-guard position, it is apparent that the right or lead hand will lose considerable punching power to a right hander. Unless he can draw his right hand further back, he lacks the space needed to deliver the most devastating blow. Power is now being replaced by speed in this case. To compensate, the left or rear hand must do the job.

If you are a natural right-hander, punching with the left seems very awkward in the beginning. You seem to be off-balance, your punch from that hand is weak, slow and not too accurate. But by constant practice with your right foot forward, as in photo A, and doing the motion exactly as the second exercise, except now using your right foot as the lead, you should develop your punching power in that hand.

Eventually, your rear straight and cross would be the most powerful punches available in your arsenal. You will be depending

on them for your knockout blows. Keep practicing with your left hand until it becomes natural.

One of the most helpful but simple implements that Bruce Lee incorporated into his training schedule was the round steel cylinder. The cylinder, weighing about a pound, fits snugly in the hand. You can quickly improve your delivery of punches by taking advantage of this exercise. Holding a pair of these cylinders in each hand, stand with your feet parallel and punch directly in front of your nose several times. The idea behind this is to develop the snapping or whipping blows. If you keep your body and arms

relaxed, you will notice that your punches will automatically snap back at the end of your delivery.

This training has a two-fold purpose. It develops speed in your delivery, as well as power. After a while you will learn to punch with heaviness in your blows even without the weights. The secret behind this is to concentrate or pretend that your empty hands still contain the cylinders as you throw the punches.

In throwing a hard punch, it is easy to develop a bad habit of throwing your shoulders out of line so only one shoulder does the work. In other words, the alignment of the shoulders can easily be disturbed; hence, loss of power in delivery. To retain the coordination between the shoulders, Lee uses a staff, as in photos 1 and 2. By holding the staff with his hands far apart, he places it on his back shoulders. As he twists his body from one position to another, the long staff keeps his shoulders straight in all the movements.

After you have practiced with the cylinder weights for some time, you will notice that your blows have more impact even without the weights. This is your introduction to the fact that your mind can do wonders to your physical strength. This extra power or strength is what Lee called the "flowing energy" or in aikido, the "ki," and in tai chi chuan, the "chi."

What you are now experiencing is just a small degree of the flowing energy. To enhance this energy, there are several exercises.

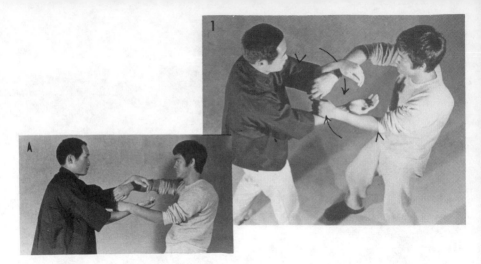

One of the best that should be an integral part of your training, is the "chi sao" which was briefly described in the chapter on balance.

In performing the chi sao to develop your energy, keep your body and arms relaxed, as in photos 1 (bird's-eye view) and A (side view). As your wrists touch your partner's as in drawing figure A, just put enough stress in your hands to roll your arms back and forth. In the following photos from 1 to 6, Lee demonstrates how your arms should be rolling. Arrows are indicated in each photo to illustrate the motion of the hands. The elbows' positions are closed to their body as they roll their arms constantly and smoothly.

The rolling motion is not the essence of chi sao. It is the flowing from your arms that is important. The idea in the early stages is not to fight each other's strength but to concentrate on getting the feel of this energy. If you attempt to shove your partner

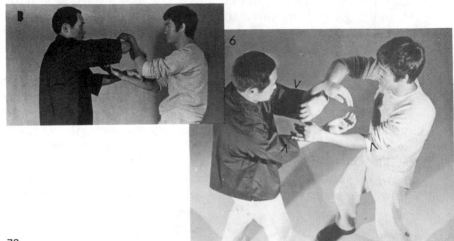

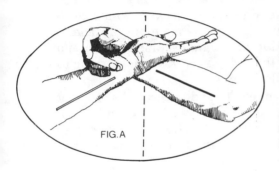

FIG.A

backward, you will be missing the whole purpose of chi sao. This forceful movement will tense your arms, and consequently your shoulders will become rigid. You will then lose your balance and begin to rely on brute strength instead of the flowing energy.

The energy must flow from the pit of your abdomen, instead of your shoulders. To do this, imagine that water is flowing through your arms like a hose, being fed from the center of your body (about) the navel. This causes the under part of your arms to become heavy. Keep your fingers loose and outstretched, as the water has to flow out from the little fingers.

If both partners emit the same degree of energy or water through their arms, neither will penetrate the other. The motion will be constant, even and rhythmic. Each partner will feel the other's arms as supple but firm. Arms look weak but they are very potent. Your elbows should be immovable—they can't be coerced toward your body. Your pliable arms can be moved from side to side but not toward your body. As you become more proficient, the circumference of your motion or rolling becomes smaller and smaller, as if the water flowing through your arms is now trying to penetrate and cover all the smaller cracks.

Chi sao is an important part of jeet kune do because its efficient application of techniques relies on looseness of arms and body. This exercise is the best way to develop your flowing of energy so you can be constantly relaxed and loose and yet not sacrifice power.

To test if your energy is flowing, have someone extend his hand to you and land a chopping blow to his hand. First, do it normally and then do it with the flowing energy—concentrate on the heaviness of your hand, keep your arm loose and place the weight at the bottom of your arm. Don't tell your partner what you are doing. After each blow ask him if he feels any difference. If he does, then hit his hand both with and without the flowing energy, letting him decide after each blow if the force is heavier or lighter. If the blows with the flowing energy are more powerful, you know you are doing it right. If you are unable to find anyone to cooperate with you, you can also test it on your own hand.

The incredible one-inch punch, as in photos 1, 2 and 3, that Lee used to awe the crowd in demonstration, was possible because of his proficient use of his hips, flowing energy, punching through and the delivering of the punch. This fist is vertical and cocked at the wrist, as in photo A. The fist turns upward suddenly at impact,

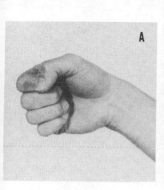

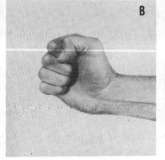

as in photo B. This vertical-fist punch is only used in close quarters from five inches or less to the target. If you attempt to use this punch from a distance, it will throw your timing off at impact.

There are other ways to amplify the power of your flowing energy. You can do it while driving your car. Place your arms on the steering wheel as though you are doing chi sao and put pressure on your arms. In photo A, it seems like Lee is doing isometric exercise but he is actually pressing his arms to the bar,

flowing his energy. Fortunately, developing your flowing energy can be practiced anywhere that allows you to put pressure on one or both arms.

Many who attempt the one-inch punch knock their opponents off their feet, but instead of punching, they only push them down. You can't hurt your opponent by a push. The art of punching is not pushing. In punching, the peak of your force or strength is at the point of contact, but in pushing, the force begins from the outset of the delivery and generally loses its power by the time your arm is fully extended. Punching comes from the rotation of your hips, while pushing is usually from the rear foot, propelling your body forward.

When you are hitting, especially the heavy bag, punch through the bag. You will find that you will have a deeper and stronger penetration if you do that instead of concentrating on the surface of the bag. Follow-through means continuous acceleration of your punch to the target. However, the momentum or power does not cease there but extends through the target. It isn't hitting your opponent but driving through him. After driving through him, your punching hand should be withdrawn as quickly as you thrust it forward.

Don't throw your punches in a windup motion; they should be thrown straight. Your fist clenches just before your whip-like impact. To add additional power, the free hand can be drawn suddenly and conjunctly toward your body at the point of impact.

If you are taking a step to throw a punch, your fist makes the contact before your foot lands on the floor; otherwise, the body weight would be assimilated onto the floor instead of behind your punch. Your hips and shoulders must initiate the action before your arm, to deliver a rapid, precise and powerful blow. Although your foot-movement adds to your power, you can actually knock out your opponent without taking a step or showing any strain in your action, if delivery was correctly done.

A powerful blow depends on leverage and timing. Right timing is a must for a powerful blow. Without it, your impact is lost in motion—it may reach too early or too late.

Pulling Power

Although Bruce Lee first studied wing chun kung fu, he improvised so many different techniques to it that jeet kune do seems to have no bearing on kung fu. Lee did not completely discard the wing chun's techniques. He retained some of them but also altered them so completely that they are not recognizable as the original art.

Two techniques he continued to practice were the "lop sao" (grabbing the hand) and "pak sao" (slapping block), especially after doing the chi sao. He was forced to revise both techniques, because in wing chun both partners stand with their bodies facing each other squarely and their feet parallel. But in the JKD

A

1

2

on-guard position the partners stand with one foot forward, and the hand extension is not the same.

Lee always felt that correct weight-training could increase his power. But he was very selective in his exercise. He avoided drills that would develop muscles which would interfere with his performance in sparring or fighting.

Besides the abdominal muscles, he concentrated heavily on his forearms because he felt that these were the muscles depended on in punching and in pulling, as in lop sao. His drills included the reverse curl. To receive the most benefit from this, he covered the bar with a sponge so he lost his gripping power as he wrapped his hands over the sponge. When doing the exercise, he depended heavily on his forearm muscles to carry the weights to his chest.

Another excellent exercise for the forearms was the reverse extension. Instead of curling his arms, he lifted the weights straight out in front of him. With his arms fully extended, he supported the weights for as long as possible at the chest level.

He also squeezed a rubber ball in his palm and worked with the wrist roller, as in photos 1 and 2. Using the dumbbell without the plates on one end, he twisted his wrist back and forth.

Lee developed such a strength in his arms that when he jerked his partner, he snapped his head backward as the body flew toward him. A contributing factor that developed the pulling power was his persistent training of lop sao on the wing chun's "dummy," as in photo A. Besides developing the forearm muscles, he also toughened his arms by slamming them into the wooden arm.

While working out with weights be sure to include speed and flexibility exercises congruently. A heavy weight lifter with a great deal of power but no flexibility or speed will have a problem hitting his opponent. It will be like a rhinoceros trying to corner a rabbit.

Power in Kicking

Striking with your foot has several advantages. First, your leg is much more powerful than your hand. Actually, kicking properly is the most powerful and damaging blow you can administer. Second, your leg is longer than your hand so it is your first line of attack, normally preceding your punch. Third, to block a kick is

1

very difficult, especially on the low-line areas like the shin, knee and groin.

Unfortunately, too many martial artists do not profit from their assets. They do kick but without any power. Flicky or pole-like kicks, as in photos 2 and 3, are still being used. They do not generate enough power to hurt or damage. In the flicky kicks your weight is not behind the blow and in the pole-like kick your body is too off-balanced.

Bruce Lee's forte was the side kick, as shown in photo A, which differs from the classical side kick. In the classical, the side thrust kick has power but no speed. The side snap kick has speed but no power. In the JKD's side kick both the snap and thrust are combined so there is no loss of power and speed. Lee used to drop a two-inch board from his shoulder height and shatter it in half before it landed on the ground. If his kick had only power but no snap, the board would be hurled at a distance without breaking, unless it was braced. If his kick had the snap but no power, the board would not break because a two-inch board without support is too thick to split with a snap kick.

To do the side kick, stand with your feet apart and parallel to each other. Lift your right foot about 12 inches from the floor as you balance on your left. Stomp your right foot straight down with force and let it snap upward about an inch from the floor. Like punching with the flowing energy, here again, you should

2

3

concentrate with heaviness in your foot. In other words, the water is now flowing through your right leg (hose) and when it is fully extended by your downward stomp (gushing of the water), it snaps upward (splashes explosively). Until you warm up your legs by light kicking, do not stomp your foot violently.

Now you are set to kick sideways. As in stomping, place all your weight on your left foot as you lift your right foot, and kick straight out instead of down. Your left knee should be bent slightly so you can lean a little backward and not forward, as most beginners do. Pivot on the ball of your left foot as you thrust your right foot forward. For the extra power, twist your hips just an instant before the full extension of your leg—it gives you the screwdriver or the twisting force in your kick. Then snap your foot at the full extension for the whipping effect.

If you like to kick something solid, you can hit any wood or concrete wall. Measure your distance to the wall and just kick it. Since your foot should be landing flat, you will not hurt yourself. A forceful kick will just bounce your body backward, as the wall will not flex.

After you have the knack of doing the side kick, you are prepared to kick the heavy bag. From the on-guard position, do the forward burst as explained in the chapter, "Footwork." Aim your blow directly at the center of the bag, as in photos 1, 2 and 3.

At impact, your foot should land horizontally on the bag, not obliquely. The sound at impact should be a loud, cracking thud like a whip if you have kicked through the bag and snapped your foot at the end. If there is more push than hit, the sound will be a light or weak thud. In both kicks there is force exerted, except the hit will do the damage and the push will just knock the opponent down innocuously.

If you lunge at the bag swiftly and keep your body in balance, you can generate more power in your kick than you ever thought possible. Generally, the kick is delivered with your body lunging close to the floor to keep you in balance even after the execution. But for a much more powerful blow, lift your body a little higher while moving toward the bag and, just as you are propelling your right foot through the bag, stomp or drive your left foot downward. In other words, the force is now being exerted from both legs. This may be the ultimate in delivering a punishing blow without a weapon.

One note of caution: If you miss the bag completely or don't hit it solidly, you can hurt your kicking knee. The reason is that your foot is hurling much faster than your body and when you miss, it is like someone jerking your leg off the knee socket.

In real fighting or sparring, it is not too practical to utilize the latter kick, as it can easily leave you off-balance if you miss. And furthermore, the higher you leap, the more time you allow your opponent to avoid your attack.

The heavy bag is one of the most valuable apparatuses in JKD and, as a matter of fact, in the other martial arts, too, because one can practice on it alone. You can have a good workout by just doing the side kicks on it continuously for several minutes. As you kick the bag, let it swing back each time before kicking it again.

To teach a beginner in kicking, hold the bag for him by placing your knee at the bottom rim of the bag and both your hands

gently behind the center area of the bag to avoid having your fingers crushed. Before you ever stand with your back facing the bag, be sure you know the strength of the kicker. In photo 1, Lee hit the bag so hard that the impact sent the person behind it flying across the room, causing an injury to his neck, which lasted for several days, from the whiplash.

Lee always believed that one should practice hitting different

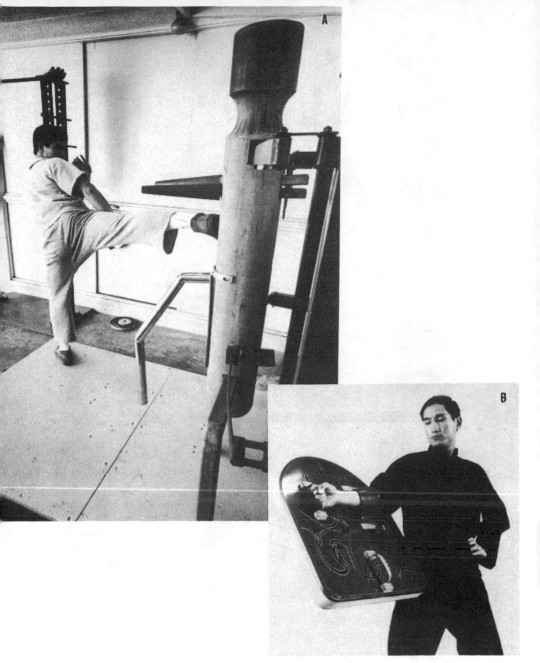

types of targets to get a different feeling from each on impact. He used the heavy bag mostly, but often kicked at the wall canvas, bean or sand bag, the punching pad, the wooden dummy, as in photo A, and the portable heavy shield, as in photo B.

After the heavy bag, Lee's next favorite apparatuses at which to kick were the heavy shield and the air bag because he could exert all his power onto a moving target without really hurting the holder, as in photos 1, 2 and 3.

Although the front kick is not as powerful as the side kick, Lee increased the explosiveness of his kick by the use of his hips. Instead of relying only on the snap of the foot from the knee, he

jerked his hips forward just an instant before his foot makes contact, as in photos A and B. The timing of this movement is very important and difficult to do. Practice it daily until you have the knack of it.

The text attempts to illustrate a step-by-step instruction of doing the side kick. But once you understand how to deliver it, you should do it without hesitation but in one smooth, fluid motion.

Chapter V
Speed Training

Speed

Speed in fighting depends not
    just on your hands and feet in swiftness,

But other attributes such as
    nontelegraphic moves and awareness.

Speed in fighting is to hit
    your foe without yourself being hit.

This can only be done by hours
    of practice and being completely fit.

Speed in fighting is no good
    without the power that goes with it.

SPEED TRAINING

What is speed in fighting? Is it the velocity of your hands, feet and body movement? Or are there other, prevalent essentials in a good fighter? What is a good fighter?

To answer these questions: A good fighter is one who can hit his opponent quicker, harder, without much perceptible effort, and yet avoid being hit. He doesn't only possess a pair of fast hands and feet or quick body movement but has other qualities such as nontelegraphic moves, good coordination, perfect balance and keen awareness. Although some people are endowed with a few of these qualities, most of these attributes are developed through hard training.

All the strength or power you have developed from your training is wasted if you are slow and can't make contact. Power and speed go hand-in-hand. A fighter needs both to be successful.

One immediate way to increase your speed at impact is to "snap" or "whip" your hand or foot just before contact. It is the same principle as the overhand throw. For example, if you throw a baseball with a full swing and snap your wrist at the last moment or the tail end of your swing, the ball will have more velocity than without the snap. Naturally, the longer swing with a snap will have more acceleration at the end than a shorter swing with a snap. A 12-foot whip, flung exactly, will generate more sting than a two-foot whip.

Speed in Punching

The back fist punch is not the quickest nor is it too strong because you are unable to utilize the total body movement. But it is one blow in which you can fully apply the whipping or snapping motion. First of all, it is thrown more like a swing than a forward thrust; that means you can put more momentum in the delivery. Second, there is more elasticity or freedom of motion in your wrist, bending it from side to side (palm to knuckles), than up and down (thumb to little finger). That means you are able to whip or snap it more vigorously, as in photo A.

The back fist is used mostly to the head section of your opponent. It is used heavily in combination with "lop sao" (grabbing-the-hand technique), as in photo B. It is delivered

from shoulder height but can also be used as a surprise attack and be launched anywhere from your waist line to your shoulder. It is very difficult to block once you have acquired the nontelegraphic moves.

Although some power is lost in this punch, it is compensated for or redeemed when combined with lop sao. If you can develop a strong pulling power in your arm, you will be able to jerk your opponent forward and apply the back fist punch. The impact should be devastating when your knuckles contact your opponent's face. It is like two fast-moving cars colliding, head on.

To develop speed or quickness in the back fist punch, light a candle and attempt to blow it out with the acceleration of your punch. Another interesting exercise is to have a partner attempt to block your punch as you throw it at his face, with control. If he

A

1

2

misses his block, you should be able to stop your punch about one-quarter inch from his skin.

Lee also used the bouncing head dummy, as in photo A, which was created strictly for solitary training. The head is padded and resilient, to take any hard blows.

The leading finger jab is the fastest attacking weapon available to you. It is fast in reaching your target because it travels only a short distance. It is also the longest hand weapon accessible to you. Since you do not clench your fist but have your fingers extended, you add several more inches to your reach, as in photos 1 and 2.

Power is not needed in this technique because you focus your aim at the eyes of your enemy. Instead, your important assets are accuracy and speed. The jab is a threatening and dangerous weapon to the adversary because it does so much damage and is so difficult to defend against.

To protect yourself from damaging your fingers, if you should ever miss and hit a hard object such as the head or a bone of your enemy, learn to form your hand properly. Align the tip of your hand, as in photo Y, by slightly bending the longer fingers to adjust to the shorter and tuck your thumb in. Your hand should resemble a spear.

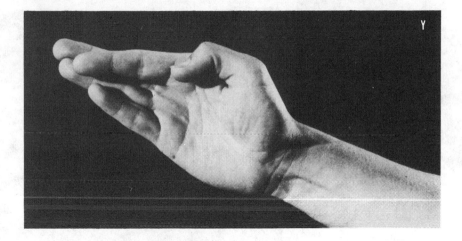

To develop speed in the finger jab, you need a great deal of practice and most of this will be the result of your own initiative. Speed relies on economy of motion and the jab is one technique with which you have the opportunity to experiment. The jab, like all the blows in JKD, must be thrust forward without any retracting motion. It is like a snake darting at its prey without warning.

The more hours you spend in speed hitting, the faster your hands will travel, as time goes by. Like the boxer who whips out his hands while jogging, you must also take solitary training seriously. One excellent training device for this is the paper target. It is so inexpensive and easy to construct and yet very valuable to

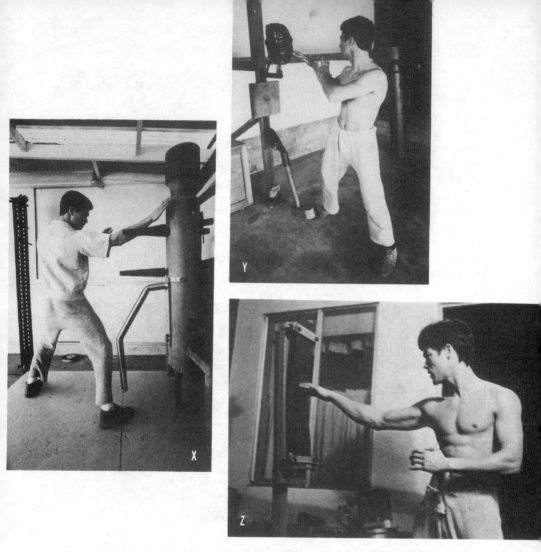

anyone who wants to enhance his speed in punching or jabbing.

Besides the paper target, Lee used to practice on a thick leather strip to toughen his fingers, as in photo Z. He also worked heavily on the bouncing head dummy, as in photo Y, which is excellent for finger jabbing. It gives when struck but is solid enough to harden the fingers.

Although the wooden dummy is too solid to jab your fingers into, it is a valuable apparatus with which to practice the finger jab combination, as in photo X. It presents almost a real-life opponent with its arms outstretched and its leg impeding your approach.

The leading finger jab is the fastest hand weapon and the leading straight is the fastest of all the punches. The leading straight is the backbone punch of jeet kune do. It is the main offensive weapon, but also an important defensive tool to stop and intercept a complex attack in an instant.

Although the leading straight punch has been discussed in the chapter on "Power Training," power is not one of its leading characteristics. Actually, the leading straight punch is more appropriately classified as a "speed" punch. Like the finger jab it travels only a short distance to the target, as in photos 1, 2 and 3, because that hand is already extended—closest to its target.

Besides being the fastest punch, the straight lead is also the most accurate because it is delivered straight forward, at a close distance, and your balance is left intact. Like the finger jab, it is hard to block, especially if you keep it in a continuous, small motion. Besides, it can be delivered faster while in motion than from a fixed position. Like the finger jab, it keeps the opponent "on edge" by its threatening gesture.

Put some "zip" into your punch by snapping it just before impact. Keep your hand loose and tighten your fist only an instant before contact. To put explosiveness in the blow, utilize the flowing-energy concept by adding heaviness to your hand.

The straight lead is not an end, but a means to an end. It is not a powerful blow that will knock your opponent flat with one punch, but it is the most dominating punch in JKD and is used profusely with the other combination punches and kicks.

The straight punch should be delivered from an on-guard position with the point of contact in line with the surface of your shoulder, as in photos 1, 2 and 3. Against a short opponent or if you are hitting at the low line level, bend your knees so your shoulders are aligned to the point of contact. Likewise, if he is a tall person, stand on the balls of your feet.

Later, as you progress, the straight punch should be thrown

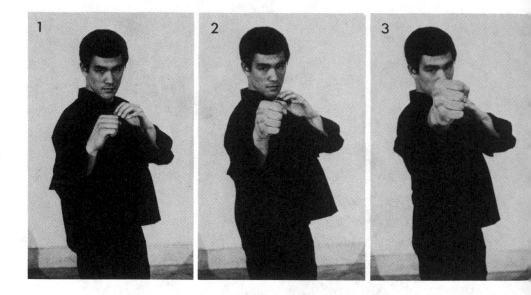

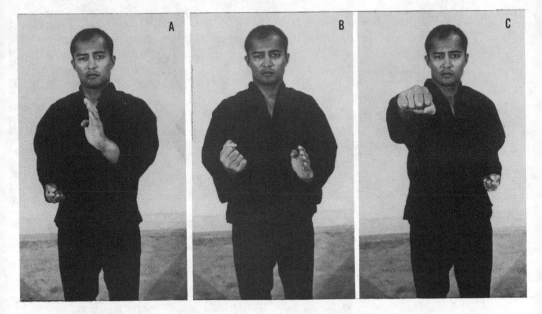

from any position in which your hand happens to be, without any extra motion, like retracting it or pulling your shoulder back before delivery. But the punch must be launched with your body in balance to be effective.

Unlike the classical stance, the hand is never placed on your hip, as in photos A, B and C, nor is the punch initiated from there. It is impractical to have your hand traveling the extra, needless distance. Furthermore, delivery of your punch from the hip exposes a large area of your body during the action.

As discussed in the last chapter, the leading right will have more sting if you pivot your hips and utilize all the other functions for a heavy blow. But sometimes this will telegraph your movement, and you have to decide whether to sacrifice speed for power. This depends on your opponent. If he is very slow and awkward, you can utilize the powerful blows and still contact. But if he is fast, you may have to concentrate on speed more than power. Among the best equipment to develop speed and accuracy in your punching, is the old-fashioned speed bag, as in photo A. The bag, supported by an elastic line to the ceiling and a rope to the floor, is suspended to your shoulder level. To use the bag properly, you have to be quick with your hands. You have to hit the target

perfectly so the bag will bounce directly back to you; and you need good timing with your hands.

In the beginning, use both hands to punch the bag and stand with your feet parallel but comfortably apart. Hit the bag directly straight, using your nose as the guiding point. The most valuable feature of the bag is that it compels you to hit directly and crisply and not push or it will not return to you sharply. But once you have the knack of punching it after several practices, you can be in the on-guard position and employ the fist-and-elbow combination. Hit with your fist and block or strike with your elbow and forearm, as in photo B.

You cannot hit the bag standing in the classical style, with your punch delivered from your hip, because it will be too late for you to react after the first punch. You are liable to be hit on your face, since your hands will not be able to protect your head from the oncoming bag.

The punching pads, as shown in photo Y, are versatile equipment, used to increase speed and heavy punching, for kicking and for applying combinations. You can work with one or two pieces.

In photos 1 and 2, Lee practices an explosive leading right punch with just one pad. Besides explosiveness, the one pad is good for developing speed to your punch. Have your partner hold out the pad and whenever you attempt to punch, he jerks it swiftly either upward or downward, trying to make you miss, as you attempt to hit it squarely.

In photos 1, 2, and 3, he throws his leading right and follows up with his left to the second pad. With a pair of pads, your partner can help you develop speed, aim and coordination by moving himself and his hands around—revealing a pair of elusive targets.

Punching the wall canvas bag is not recommended for speed. To develop speed, you must hit with speed in mind and not power. If

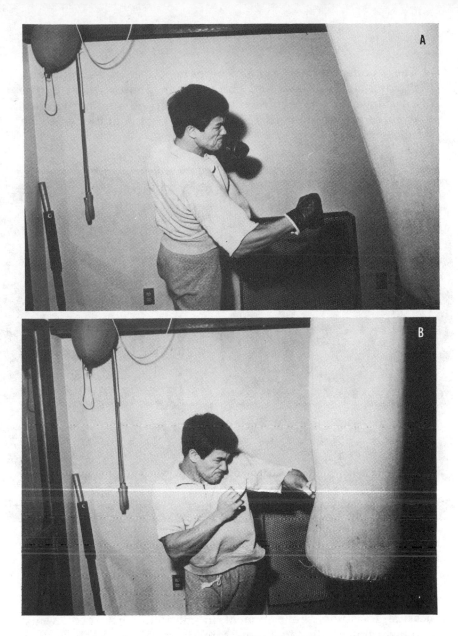

you hit with full power all the time, you will be sacrificing speed. Even while hitting the heavy bag, as in photos A and B, you can hit with a combination of speed and power. Use your dominating, leading hand mostly for speed and your rear hand for power. From time to time you can throw heavy punches from both hands as you "crowd" the bag.

The wooden dummy can also be used to learn speed punching with combination blows and parries, as in photos A and B. The disadvantage for one who hasn't worked on the dummy before is that he can injure himself if his fists are not conditioned to hit solid objects.

A   B

The lead is almost like the leading straight punch, except that it lacks the force of the latter punch. It is used mostly as a "feeler" in the early rounds of sparring or in the beginning of a fight between two crafty fighters. The lead jab is used as a cautious measure to study the opponent in motion. When two evenly matched, skilled fighters meet, sometimes the lead jab is used throughout the fight.

The lead jab is generally the dominating hand technique in boxing, but in JKD it is the leading straight punch. Both techniques have almost the same features: fast, accurate, short delivery, body balance in delivery, and both are hard to block.

In offense, the lead jab is used to keep the opponent off-balance and to create openings for more punishing blows. In defense, it is an effective maneuver to stop or meet an attack. For example, you can "beat your opponent to the punch" by throwing a quick jab to his face just as he is about to launch an attack. The jab can also be delivered from an extended arm to "stiff-arm" or keep your opponent at a distance—prevent him from close-in fighting.

The jab is mostly focused on the face because it lacks force and does little damage to the body. It is a weaker, pestering stroke, good for a stratagem. It is thrown with looseness in your arm and a snap before impact.

An excellent child's game that is fun and can be played with anyone, is the "slapping" match. Extend your arm fully in front of you with your hand outstretched. Your thumb is on the top as you hold it vertically. When your partner swings his hand to slap yours, you react by jerking it suddenly upward and toward you, trying your best to avoid contact. You let him do the slapping until he misses, then you reverse roles.

Nontelegraphic Punch

One of the most distinctive features that sets JKD apart from the classical styles of kung fu and boxing is that Bruce Lee incorporated the nontelegraphic aspects of fencing. By adopting part of their footwork and applying the principle of thrusting the hand before your body, it is almost impossible to parry or block the speed punches such as the back fist, jab or the lead punch.

The concept behind this is that if you initiate your punch without any forewarning such as tensing your shoulders, moving your foot or body, the opponent will not have enough time to react. When he sees the punch coming—that is, if he ever sees it—it will be too late for him to block or parry it. Actually, the punch already makes contact and your hand is snapping back when your body edges forward. It is the exact movement of the fencer who thrusts his foil forward and does not move forward until his hand is being retracted.

If you punch simultaneously, with just a slight motion of your feet or body, you have already telegraphed or warned your opponent of your intention. The secret in the nontelegraphic moves is to relax your body and arms but keep them weaving in a

slight motion. Whip out your hand loosely so your shoulders don't tense and clench your hand just an instant before contact, as you snap it. You have to keep a "poker face" while facing your opponent. A slight twitch or expression on your face may trigger your intention and warn your opponent.

Lee was so good in speed punching that he had a problem getting volunteers to come to him when he demonstrated in karate tournaments. Even the champions were afraid to confront him because most of them knew of his prowess with his hands. In photos 1 and 2, Lee demonstrated his speed against a karate black belt. Even after indicating to the volunteer where his punching would be directed, the black belt was unable to block his punch in eight tries. Lee was successful, not just because of his quick hands but because of his flawless, nontelegraphic movement.

Use your nontelegraphic punch with your forward shuffle as discussed in the chapter on "Footwork." Practice the back fist first, then the finger jab and finally the leading straight punch.

In the beginning, punch or jab into the air and subsequently upon the paper target. Later, use the punching pad. Like training in speed punching, have your partner jerk the pad quickly when you throw your punch, trying his utmost to make you miss it.

Another exercise that you can include in your training is the "clapping" game. Stand about a full arm's length plus another four or five inches away from him. Let your partner keep his hands about a foot apart in front of him. The idea is to throw a punch to his face or body straight between his hands. It is a test as to whether you can hit the target and snap your fist before he can clap it between his hands.

If he can't, then let him reduce the distance between his hands until it is only about six inches. You can also step further away from him in delivering your punch. But before you attempt to do this drill, be sure that you can control your punch. If he misses your blow, you should be able to stop your punch above the surface of his skin.

It may be wise to learn control in punching first, before you attempt the clapping exercise. Have your partner stand motionless; throw your punches about two inches from his face. Then gradually throw your punch closer and closer until you are barely touching his skin. Your partner should only feel the draft from your action. In the meantime, your partner can learn not to blink as the blow almost brushes his face.

A

112

Speed in Kicking

The most dominating kicks in JKD are the side and hook kicks. The side kick can be used with quickness and power while the hook kick is used mostly for speed. In JKD most of the kicks are launched from the leading foot, shortening the distance between yourself and the target.

The hook kick is focused generally on the upper line—from the waist to the head. It is especially effective when directed to the ribs of your opponent, just below his arm, as in photo A. As mentioned in the previous chapter, the leg is stronger than the hand so even a fast kick like the hook can disable your opponent with just one blow.

The hook kick is more difficult to learn than the side kick because it is harder to deliver, and it tends to throw you off-balance in the process, especially on the high kicks.

To do the hook kick, stand in the on-guard position, as in photo 1. Lift your lead knee until your thigh is horizontal, as in photo 2. Your leg below the knee should be hung loosely pointing to the floor at about 45 degrees. Your weight should be completely on the rear foot with the knee slightly bent, and your body leaning backward. Then pivot on the ball of your rear foot, which automatically induces your hips to rotate. Finally snap your foot from the knee which straightens the supporting leg, as in photos 3 and 4. The hook kick is performed with just one motion from the time your foot leaves the floor. Your eyes should be constantly on the target and your kick is aimed not at the surface of the target but through it. Your foot, like the punch, should snap or whip just prior to impact.

One fault of a beginner is that he leans too far forward and

PATH OF FOOT

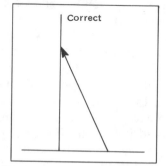

Correct

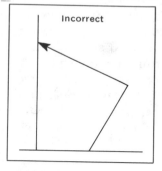

Incorrect

includes two motions in his hook kick. After raising his knee, he has a tendency to swing his foot back to deliver the kick. See chart on the path of your foot. It slows down delivery and the two motions weaken his blow because of the hesitation and the fact that he does not completely utilize the combined force of the hip and leg action, as Lee demonstrates in photos A,B,C,D.

The hook kick is usually delivered with the quick, advance

footwork. From the on-guard position, as in photo 1, step forward about three inches, as in photo 2, then slide your rear foot quickly forward, as in photo 3. Just before your rear foot contacts the front, lift your front foot to apply the kick, as in photo 4.

Sometimes your opponent may "crowd" you and you find yourself quite close to him. In this kind of predicament, omit the three-inch step and, instead, from the on-guard position, as in

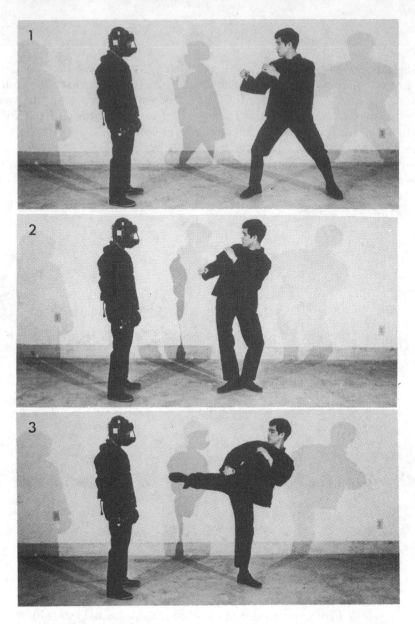

photo 1, slide your rear foot quickly forward just behind the front foot, as in photo 2. Then before your opponent can react, you should be launching your side kick, as in photo 3. This movement should be done with one fluid motion—no hesitation or jerkiness in between.

Other times you may find yourself caught at intervals. You may

be too close to your opponent to take the three-inch step and too far to use the short slide, as in photo 2. When you are in that position, just do the forward burst or lunge, as in photo Y, before delivering the side kick.

Although the hook kick is generally used for the upper line attack, often it is aimed at the groin area, as in photos A and B. This depends on the angle of your body to your opponent's.

Many times you will learn that it is the only practical kick to reach the hard-to-hit areas.

There are several apparatuses you can train on to develop your hook kick. One of the most practical and least expensive is the paper target. From an on-guard position, kick the target at first without stepping off. Get the "feel" of your stance (your balance) and the path of your foot. Pay close attention to the snap at impact.

Gradually kick into harder objects such as the light bag, as in photo A, and the heavy bag. For combination hand and foot techniques, use the wooden dummy, as in photo B. Once you have acquired the knack of delivering the hook kick automatically, practice with a moving target such as the punching pad. In the beginning, just use one; then later incorporate the other so you can drill both your left and right foot.

Although your instep is generally the point of contact in the hook kick, other regions of your foot can be used, such as the ball, toe and shin. But avoid using the toe and ball if you are sparring barefoot.

In most hitting, the powerful blows are usually slower than the lighter ones. But the side kick, which is the hardest blow you can release, is also a fast kick. If directed toward the low line such as the opponent's knee or shin, as in photos 1 and 2, it can be just as swift as the hook kick. Bruce Lee used to do his low-line side kicks almost as rapidly as throwing his leading jab. It was fascinating to see him chase his opponent who was reeling backward, completely off-balance.

To develop a speed side kick, stand in the on-guard position and

imagine that your opponent's leading leg is in front of you. Keep your eyes focused at your imaginary foe's face as you deliver a series of side kicks angling downward. The idea of this drill is to thrust your foot strongly but with speed and snap. The wooden dummy can also be used to practice the low side kick, as in photo A, or in combination with hand or other foot techniques.

Another fast kick is the front or the upward groin kick. It is delivered almost exactly as the hook kick. Instead of the kick being directed to the side of your opponent so your foot travels obliquely, the kick is to the groin and travels straight upward or vertically. If used with your hip motion, as discussed in the chapter on "Power Training," you can generate a much more powerful blow than the hook kick.

The front kick is not employed too often in JKD sparring because the on-guard stance doesn't allow too many opportunities for its use. But it is an effective weapon against many fighters who don't protect their groin area well.

Although the ball or toe of your foot can be the point of contact, predominantly the instep and shin are used. It can be delivered more accurately than with the toe or ball. Your foot will be traveling upward between your opponent's legs, as in photos 1 and 2. It is almost impossible to miss the target.

In sparring, infrequently you do have an opportunity to use the front kick. For example, after avoiding an attack, you may be able to swing your opponent around so his back faces you, as in photos A and B.

For your daily training, you can practice the front kick by hitting the bottom rim of a heavy bag. Other light bags or balls that can be suspended from the ceiling are excellent for practicing your skill against a moving object. The punching pad can be employed, too, by having your partner hold it horizontally with his palm facing the floor. Like the other techniques, the wooden dummy is used for combinations, as in photo Y, but you can't kick it too hard without risking injury to your foot.

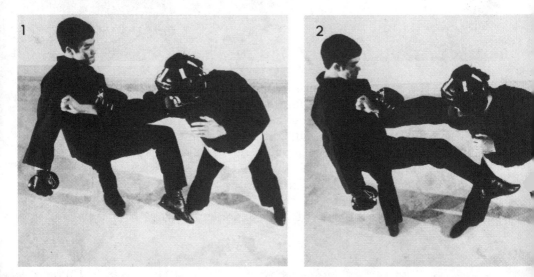

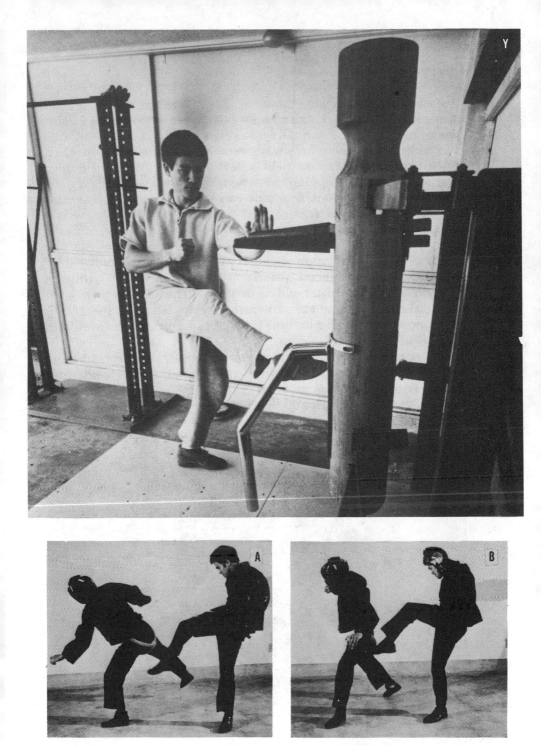

Awareness

Some athletes seem to have peripheral vision in greater dimension than others, like a basketball player who seems to know where each player is and always seems to find the open man; or a football quarterback who always sees the unguarded pass-receiver. Some experts in the sports field believe that the exceptionally high degree of peripheral vision possessed by a few athletes is innate. But they also feel that this trait can be broadened by everyone through constant practice.

In martial arts you may not need as wide a range of vision as in the other sports if you are confronted by a single person. But you surely need it when surrounded by two or more attackers.

To develop peripheral vision, focus your eyes at a distant structure, such as a high building or a pole. Then diffuse your sight so you can still see the structure clearly but also the blurry environment bordering it. Take note of any movements from both corners of your eyes.

In training, work with three or more persons and spread them out. Your eyes seem to focus on the person in the middle but your vision is actually upon all of them. As one of them moves, no matter how slightly, call out his name.

Against one opponent, your eyes should be fixed on his eyes but your vision should encompass his whole body, as in photo A. Your vision sphere is more extensive when focused at a distance

A

and as you focus your sight closer, your sphere becomes smaller. Against an individual it is harder to follow his hand motion, even if the hands are closer to your eyes than the feet, because the hand is slower.

One high-ranking martial artist was amazed at Bruce Lee's quick hand and foot reaction. Lee had the inclination to kick just before his opponent and punch just before his opponent did. To those who saw him for the first time, he seemed to have an instinct or a sixth sense that let him read other people's minds. It could be frustrating to spar with someone like him because he was upon you before you could even blink your eye.

The secret of Lee's quick reaction was his highly-developed sense of awareness, cultivated by years of training. It complemented his hand and foot techniques. Just the acceleration of your foot and hand doesn't necessarily mean that you will beat your opponent to the punch or kick. In other words, speed alone doesn't guarantee that your blow will reach your opponent before his reaches you. But by cultivating your keen sense of awareness, your chance of beating him is enhanced tremendously.

How does one develop his keen awareness? One way is to be alert to your surroundings. Learn to react quickly. For instance, while in a restaurant or other public place, select a person from the crowd and follow his movement. Whenever he or she gesticulates, you respond by a silent "ugh" or any other quiet, sharp sound. Gradually, increase your response by attempting to anticipate or beat his gesture with an "ugh."

If you have a dog, practice keen awareness by holding a rag before him. Whenever he jumps for it, react with an "ugh" as you simultaneously jerk the rag from his grasp. At the outset, hold the rag high, but as your reaction quickens, lower it toward him. You will be surprised how much this simple exercise can shorten your response-time.

If you aren't convinced, do the same exercise without the sound and, instead, just jerk the rag away. You will then realize how slow your reaction can be.

An exercise that you can do with your partner is allowing him to gesticulate quickly as you react to him. Then later, hold the punching pad in front of him and let him hit it. As he throws his speed punch, jerk your hand quickly with a simultaneous "ugh." Incredibly, this simple exercise can add a great deal of speed to your punch and kick.

More Bruce Lee Books from Ohara

TAO OF JEET KUNE DO
by Bruce Lee. Code No. 401

BRUCE LEE'S FIGHTING METHOD Vol. 1: Self-Defense Techniques
by Bruce Lee and M. Uyehara. Code No. 402

BRUCE LEE'S FIGHTING METHOD Vol. 2: Basic Training
by Bruce Lee and M. Uyehara. Code No. 403

BRUCE LEE'S FIGHTING METHOD Vol. 3: Skill in Techniques
by Bruce Lee and M. Uyehara. Code No. 404

BRUCE LEE'S FIGHTING METHOD Vol. 4: Advanced Techniques
by Bruce Lee and M. Uyehara. Code No. 405

CHINESE GUNG FU
by Bruce Lee. Code No. 451

THE LEGENDARY BRUCE LEE
by the Editors of Black Belt magazine. *Code No. 446*

THE BRUCE LEE STORY
by Linda Lee. Code No. 460

THE INCOMPARABLE FIGHTER
by M. Uyehara. Code No. 461

OHARA ▥ PUBLICATIONS, INC., 24715 Ave. Rockefeller, P.O. Box 918, Santa Clarita, CA 91380-9018

BRUCE LEE-1940-1973

Bruce Lee flashed brilliantly like a meteor through the world of martial arts and motion pictures. Then, on July 20, 1973, in Hong Kong, like a meteor—he vanished, extinguished by sudden death. He was just 32.

Bruce Lee began his martial arts studies with wing chun, under the tutelage of the late Yip Man, to alleviate the personal insecurity instilled by Hong Kong city life. Perhaps because his training enveloped him to the point of fanaticism, he was eventually able to refine, distill and mature into a philosopher, technician and innovator of the martial arts.

After intensive study of different martial arts styles and theories, Lee developed a concept of martial arts for the individual man. This concept he later labeled Jeet Kune Do, the way of the intercepting fist. It has antecedents not only in his physical training and voluminous martial arts library (over two thousand books), but in his formal education as well (a philosophy major at the University of Washington, Seattle).

Lee also combined his martial arts expertise with his knowledge of acting skills and cinematic techniques, starring in several motion pictures: *The Big Boss*, *Fists of Fury*, *Way of the Dragon* and *Enter the Dragon*.

Bruce Lee's death plunged both martial arts and film enthusiasts into an abyss of disbelief. Out of their growing demand to know more of and about him, his *Tao of Jeet Kune Do* was published—which is now followed by BRUCE LEE'S FIGHTING METHOD.

This second in a series of volumes, which has been compiled and organized by his longtime friend, M. Uyehara, utilizes some of the many thousands of pictures from Lee's personal photo files. Uyehara is a former student of Bruce Lee.